NI CITY PROSE

Confessions of a 1980s Kid

CHRIS ANTHONY

CMLLC ENTERTAINMENT

NEW YORK   LOS ANGELES

CMLLC ENTERTAINMENT

11333 MOORPARK STREET
STUDIO CITY, CA 91602

for my baby
JUNE

This book is dedicated to all of
the artists that antagonize societal
conventions and norms to express
themselves.

Thank you.

TABLE OF CONTENTS

INTRODUCTION

Thank you for taking this journey and reading my version of some of the events and history that shaped me as an artist and a person growing up in New York City in the 1980s. The word "history" is interesting in its root meaning because it literally means someone's story. And this is mine.

There are many tales in here that involve graffiti and the lifestyle that entailed, but even if you did not write graffiti but grew up in New York City at that time or are just interested in New York history, graffiti was a part of that city undeniably. Mayor Ed Koch spoke of it often, if you commuted to work you couldn't miss it. This book will give you insight into what it took for kids to get their names on those trains and in the city around you.

Graffiti influenced many major artists in New York City at the time, Andy Warhol, Jean-Michel Basquiat and Keith Haring are just a few. Graffiti eventually grew into mainstream pop culture and today it is exploited by many of the top brands in the world including Nike, Adidas, Balenciaga, Louis Vuitton, The GAP, and others, without any knowledge of where it came from or how many people suffered and died making it an art.

This book is written in prose and the stories are told "On the block" style as if we were telling them to each other. It was not my intention to develop a strict chronological biography written in complex grammatical structure following any sort of rules. It is more enjoyable this way to write, and it is much more enjoyable to read, and it offers additional insight into the mindset of a kid growing up in New York City in the 1980s. When writing some of these entries I meditated and went back into the moment of my childhood, the result is sometimes a childlike voice telling the story, this was my voice at the time. I did not adjust the voice to be my voice now as my voice then was the voice of these stories.

I feel a bit naked in this book, I'm opening up some parts of myself and my feelings that few know about, some stories never before told, there is a feeling of vulnerability that comes with this kind of biographical artwork and telling of times as we were transitioning from teens into adulthood. New York meant all of that to me. It is the city that built me, it is the city that made me strong and ready to take on the world, it is also the city that was tough, so tough at times that by the time I graduated college in the late 90's the only thing I wanted to do was leave the city I loved.

Soon after I left, New York City would be attacked on 9/11 and I was in Los Angeles when that happened. I have never forgiven myself for not being there at my city's darkest hour, the time the city needed me the most. What became apparent to me then was that no matter where or for how long I live outside of the city, I will always be a New Yorker through and through. That's not being snobby and that's not saying if you aren't a New Yorker we are better than you, not at all, sometimes the contrary. There is a degree of insecurity in growing up the way I grew up and I wear that on my face, in my vernacular, my accent and overall demeanor. It never fails when I travel or at home in Los Angeles, within the first few sentences of any conversation, for work or pleasure, the other person says to me "You grew up in New York right?" At first that didn't bother me, but the more I thought about that question, it did. Does sounding like you grew up in New York mean you sound like you have an Ivy League Education? No, obviously not. It has been a means for people to make a preconceived notion about me the second they meet me. My wife's accent is not nearly as bad as mine, she grew up at home and in school. I learned to speak on the street, on the block, and people laugh as they ask me if I've been to the Jersey Shore or tell me I sound like a character on the Sopranos. But it's not funny.

And still, I wear this moniker with pride. I am and will always be a New Yorker.

This book is a confession of sorts, I confess to some thoughts and ways of life for myself and some of us. Some confessions might be minor crimes, most are just kids being kids. I am not confessing however to any serious crimes, or any disgusting events that I may have witnessed and played no part in. Some parts of the dark city are just better left covered by the dirt that buried some of us.

I am also not telling anyone else's stories here either, those are not mine to tell. Some stories that might be embarrassing to others I will not even go near, it's not my place. This is a feel-good book in the sense that we survived this madness. It's a coming-of-age tale of a kid and other kids growing up in a city that averaged close to 2000 murders per year, kids that spent night after night on those mean streets in the toughest parts of the city. Some participants in my life mentioned in my book have had their names changed, some out of respect, some that have told me they didn't want their names mentioned even back in the day when we, or others told stories on the block. Most places and details have been left unchanged; most names are unchanged. There will not be a lot of physical descriptors of people either, these are real people with real feelings, I don't want anyone coming to get me because I made them sound fat. Smile!

This book will give you a glimpse into what it was like. There are too many stories to include, I edited it down to these stories that you'll find contained in these pages, some of them not chosen because they were better than others, some chosen just because they represented a different aspect of our youth. There are enough stories for a second book, probably even a third.

Years before I was born there was a TV Show called -

"There Are 8 Million Stories in a Naked City".

These are eighteen of mine.

Chapter 1

THE TOWN BY THE BAY

Bayside Queens was the town where we lived and grew up. A middle class almost exclusively blue-collar neighborhood segregated by race, nationality, and religion from block to block, that sat between the richer neighborhoods of Long Island a few miles to the east and the urban centers of New York City a few miles to the west.

The town of Bayside was neither here nor there and we were surely tougher than the long island kids to east and probably out of our league with the city kids to the west, leaving us with an enormous chip on our shoulders and something to prove, apparent from a very young age.

Bayside, as it was named, sat on the West shore of Little

Neck Bay, just across from Great Neck Long Island to the East and the Bronx to the North. The part of Bayside where I lived was separated from the shore only by a large park called Crocheron Park, and a highway that ran along the bay called the Cross Island Parkway.

The landscape was interesting as where the park ended before the highway there was a 125 or so foot elevation change down to sea level, where the highway sat along the shore. At the edge of that side of the park there were treacherous hills known as "the cliffs" locally. They weren't quite cliffs technically, but if you fell in you would tumble down, and still could be very dangerous, but there wasn't a sheer faced drop.

"The cliffs" were definitely an outlying area where out-lying things would occur, stolen cars were often pushed down the cliffs and burned, satanic rituals happened back there, we'd find dirty torn underwear, tons of por-nography of all sorts, empty ammunition casings, you name it, all at the ripe old age of not even 10 yet.

Crocheron Park was a park loaded with "paths" that led away from the paved and public areas through all sorts of seedy under bellies. One such path went through the thick brush separating the top of the cliffs to the paved park area, and that path followed the whole top rim, and back there, even during broad daylight it was no man's land. Like much of NYC in the 70's into the early 80's back here was desolate, and if you did see anyone back there it was quite likely that someone was a creep.

Us 10 year olds and pre-teens excluded of course, al-though if you show kids something often enough it will normalize and their ability to accept and/or face what would be gasp inducing to adults today became part of our normal lives as children.

The core group of us all went to catholic school, but you didn't learn to fight and survive in catholic school, you learned to fight back here by the cliffs, and at the ends of other paths beaten into the landscape by outlying citizens mostly twice our age and older.

And where were our parents during all of this?

Working.

My dad would leave the house every single day at 5:15am, pick up his friend Jerry, who lived about five miles from us, and they would carpool beating the commuter rush hour into Manhattan from Bayside. Bayside was only about 11 miles from mid-town Manhattan but by 8am that 11 mile commute was an easy 1 ½ hours of blood boiling furious traffic. One time when I was a little bit older and had a part time job at a pet food company in NYC (Court ordered), he and Jerry would drive me home with them. And some lady cut them off and they got into it at the light, and my dad told her to "shut the car off, take your keys, and throw them into that storm grate and never drive again". It wasn't an overly vicious confrontation but was the type of thing that would happen on a daily basis in NYC traffic.

My dad did this 5:15am and return at 7pm, 5 days a week and sometimes Saturday, except on Saturdays he would leave at 7am. My mom would leave the house every day at 9am after we left for school and go to her book keeping job at a plastics company in Jamaica Queens. She would returning around 5pm, except on Tuesdays and Thursdays when she went straight to bingo and gambling until 10pm. She would often pick us up on her lunch hour and drive us home from school before heading back.

From 9 years old on. Me and my brother entirely on our own to roam the streets with the rest of the working class kids left alone to fend for themselves in a very strange, isolated and dark world.

We grew up quick.

In 1982 my dad thought it would be a good idea, because we asked him, to get us a Honda 50cc minibike, a gasoline powered dirt-bike, although be it a small one. We were 9 and 11. And we bought it from two crazy brothers that lived a block behind us, and my dad did not think it was necessary to buy us helmets. Never mind helmets on bicycles and skateboards back then, the thought of a helmet or any safety equipment for anything was just not even a consideration.

The logic of buying a dirt-bike for two kids that live in the city limits with no legal place to ride within an hour's car drive is strange now looking back, but then it seemed completely normal. We just got on the bike on the public streets and rode off and my dad just waved bye to us and went inside and didn't give it a second thought. No parents, did, it was just life, we were all just living.

But that's not to say there weren't real consequences to

any of this, we lived across the street from Crocheron Park, as I mentioned earlier, a heavily wooded multi acre park that separated a black neighborhood from a white neighborhood, only by about 100 yards. And on the black and Irish side there were a number of "group homes" that housed children and teens from families where the mothers and fathers that were not around for one reason or another. We got along well with most of them and we all hung out quite often.

In keeping with the things that kids had that just made no sense, we somehow all had CO_2 BB Gun pistols that could put your eye out, and break the skin and kill small animals, worse than that they were exact replicas of real handguns. These were commonplace in my neighborhood and seeing children running around with them was not strange, adults wouldn't even give it a second thought if they saw it. But they didn't see it because like in the cartoon "The Peanuts", there were never adults around. It was just kids raising other kids and ruling with brawn and discipline comparable to Lord of the Flies in many instances.

In one of these group homes lived this kid David. He was a fairly quiet but reputable teen that went by the street name "Ledge", short for Knowledge. I believe a religious reference of some sort, at least I always believed that but never was entirely sure or gave it much thought now looking back.

He was a nice enough kid, but he would borrow a BB Gun from a local kid named Stevie. This kid "Ledge", David, would use that BB Gun to commit an armed robbery of the Northern Blvd. Burger King on a Friday

15

Night near our house, and would be shot and killed by the police in the process.

One of us, killed with the same BB Gun we all had, and this was barely a tragedy at the ripe old age of 12 years for us.

Life immediately went on. The dark underbelly of society went on, and when I say we were all just "Living", please don't mistake me for meaning "Enjoying life". Because life wasn't something to be enjoyed, the way we think of it now. People didn't consider things like work/life balance back then. It was enjoyed, but in a different way, it was a game of survival. We enjoyed surviving, we enjoyed "getting over."

We all ate in that Burger King weekly for the next decade, bullet holes still visible in the walls from that fateful night when David was shot and killed. And the holes just became part of the decor, the horror of those kinds of things always became normalized.

Looking back now the racism that existed where I grew up was real, never mind the segregation, but the segregation I always found less problematic since often groups chose to live in areas where others of their race, religion or nationality lived, and they segregated themselves so to speak. Often times though segregation occurred by economic status which tended to accumulate poorer people in certain area, that is a bit more problematic.

And the racism went all ways, but obviously it was always colder when it went from higher up on the social ladder downward.

One of our best friends was a kid named Gibson from the other side of the park, a pocket of streets with very modest houses that was diagonally Southwest from my house. The remaining perimeter was somewhat wealthier families, and nicer houses and the bay.

On the white side of the park there was a palpable attitude if the kids from just three blocks away were walking around. It was tangible enough that you almost never saw kids from that side of the park, just three blocks away, walking around on the white side.

Gibson used to come over to our house and hang out almost every day. And Gibson loved roller hockey, and we'd all play roller hockey in the schoolyard of PS41 across the street from the Crocheron basketball court. Both which lied directly midway between the black side of the park and the white side. And when we'd play roller hockey, other black kids that were walking to the basketball court used to stick their heads to the gate and yell things to Gibson about the basketball court being over here and to stop hanging out with us.

And Gibson used to also get that sentiment at home, and it culminated in one night at our good friend Jimmy's house, it was Gibson and about eight of us hanging out all day as the day turned to night after the summer and it is getting very cold quickly, so we all went into Jimmy's house.

Jimmy's brother Michael was there, an amazing human being and Fordham college student, and when we all got into Jimmy's house Michael put on the TV for us, again, no parents around, there were never any parents around. Just Michael who might have been 19 at the time.

Once we were all settled and watching TV, Michael looked around and said

"Hey wait a minute guys, where's Gibson?"

Being kids we were numb to any concern and just shrugged and didn't even really care about the question, upon further pressing Jimmy responded to Michael, "guess he left".

"Left? He was just here when we came in" Said Michael …we shrugged again.

Gibson was told by his father that the white people didn't want him hanging around at their houses. And Gibson felt awkward when we went inside. Michael caught up with him; Gibson returned.

But yeah, Gibson got it on all sides, and yeah Michael was a special kind of person in a crazy place. Unfortunately, Michael would die of Lymphoma just a short time later leaving a hole in Jimmy's heart for years to come.

Feels weird wrting about some of this stuff today, like maybe its not my place to even tell these stories but New York City of the 1970s and 1980s was very race conscious, and the racism was significant now looking back.

The high school near us was called "Bayside High School", no, not the one from "Saved by the Bell."

There was a part of Queens called Jamaica about five miles to the south of Bayside, and it had a sister school, Jamaica High School. Built at the same time and both built in fantastic limestone and architectural detail. Both impressive buildings. Jamaica had a much higher black polulation than Bayside. In the 1970's they started bussing kids from Jamaica to attend Bayside High School in large numbers as an attempt to desegregate neighborhoods and schools. Bayside High would have a black student population of about 50% despite being in a mostly white area.

The city bus that ran that school bussing was the Q31 bus line and it ran nonstop from near Jamaica High all the way to the front of Bayside High, coming down Francis Lewis Blvd and turning up 32nd Ave. The pocket of 32nd Ave where the bus dropped off and picked up the kids from Jamaica was heavily Italian and Irish. Very much one of those "What are you doing around here?" type of neighborhoods Spike Lee would model many of his movies about. Real shady tough types hanging around always.

There was a pizzeria on the corner called Vinny's. Diagonally across from the Q31 bus stop in front of Eldees which was a large electronics store. Eldees had a huge white wall behind the bus stop and in 1984 someone wrote in black spray paint in HUGE letters taking up half the block "Q31 back to Africa" immediately adjacent to the bus stop. It could not be missed if you were taking that bus or coming down the bus route.

The writing on that wall stayed there for five years! For five years no one thought to paint over it, no one in the community thought it might be a good idea to remove it so the kids that wait for the bus there by the dozens at a time wouldn't have to endure that insult.

And at the time, as a 13 year old kid myself, none of us really gave it that much thought either. We for sure knew it was there but like so much else, found ourselves indifferent and with other things on our mind.

Another thing that I cannot forget was the first time I saw a "Vote for Giuli, not the m**li" bumper sticker on a car when Dinkins was running against Giuliani for Mayor in the early 1990s. I saw several of these and it blows my mind in retrospect.

BROKEN BOTTLES AND THE VIETNAM MEMORIAL

Crocheron Park, was mostly referred to as "The Park" since it was central to our lives for most of it growing up. Or just Crocheron. So much of our childhoods went down either in or nearby the park ...

It consisted of two parks joined together in about the early 1900's I would guess, there was John Golden Park, not sure who he was, but his part of the park was completely sealed in with a gothic looking brick post and spiked wrought iron fencing about 8' tall, that ran about a quarter mile along the 215 street side of the park to a beautifully accented double post and huge iron gate opening. The gates were indeed closeable and lockable and looked as though they once protected an estate

20

overlooking the bay of many acres, which they probably did, and I would guess that was John Golden, some captain of industry at the industrial revolution and turn of the 19th into the 20th century. I believe it was some sort of Great Gatsby-esque resort that hosted parties overlooking the bay.

There were no remnants of an estate however, at least not in building, and looking back now there definitely were in terms of grounds layout, but we'll get to that.

If you went down 215th street along that wrought iron fencing the first opening in the gate is for a large parking lot that could hold a hundred cars. This was the setting for the one of the upcoming stories in this book, "New Snow", where Trent crashed his dad's car.

Continuing down 215th so the fencing was on your right, there is another entry gate and you could turn right again, but only on foot. As there was a wooded area that looked like it grew over a private drive or street, that ran all the way down to the bay and the backside of the park. There was a log buried in the overgrown bush preventing cars from turning down. People did find a way to get stolen cars down there sometimes though, probably by coming out one of the pedestrian gates from the park and avoiding the log.

Continuing further on 215th street, passing the over grown private drive, there was a neighborhood again of houses, more wealthy houses that became its own pocket of streets and dead ends that ran up behind the private wooded drive I just mentioned. And these houses had mafia murders and other tales of lore from the 60s and 70s into the 80s. These houses all backed up to a "Yacht club" which backed up to another foot bridge that went over the Cross Island Parkway that now separated the backside of the park and any houses from the Little Neck Bay, this was farther to the North than the "Cliffs" at the back of the Park which also had a footbridge.

It was a very impressive area in layout and geography alone. Immediately across the bay was Great Neck Long Island, which was very rich and to the left of that, separated by another water way, was The Bronx. I mean this was sort of smack dab in the middle of the edge of New York City, yet it looked almost like a rural area.

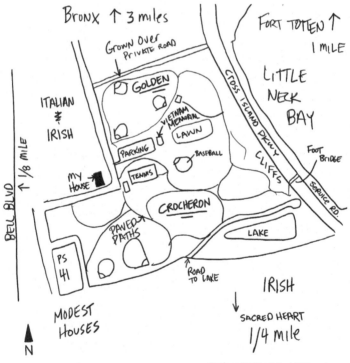

Crocheron/Golden Parks c. 1980s

22

The two parks formed an upside down L shape with the larger tall part of the L being Crocheron and the shorter part being Golden. Almost directly across the street from the house where my dad moved us in 1979 was "The Park House" which is where the parks department for the park operated, there were 8 tennis courts adjacent to the Golden parking lot, that were fenced in and closely maintained by this park house.

This was the only thing rigorously maintained in all of the 75 or so acres of the park. There were several other buildings in the park that housed bathrooms and such but all locked up tight since the 60s when they became over run with junkies and perverts and god only knows what else. They would remain locked up tight until the end of the 90s when I would finally leave New York for Los Angeles.

In fact, I still have never seen them open till this day, although by the turn of the 21st century they may have been opened once I left.

At the back of the Golden Parking lot, stood a tall obelisk much like the Washington monument. It was obviously not as big but was probably about 20 feet tall, and had a concrete rotunda of benches with bushes surrounding it. Etched on it were the names of thousands of soldiers that died in the Vietnam war, at least we always thought it was the Vietnam war, to this day I have never researched it to confirm, but the mere existence of it at that time now challenges which war it represented because I know that to have been there since 1979 when I first saw it. The Vietnam war ending in or about 1976 so it was definitely a quick turn around time for a memorial to be built back then, given procurement time for funding, approvals, etc. But maybe it was privately donated, and I do seem to recall it saying Vietnam war on it.

But what war that memorial was for was neither here nor there in this story or my childhood. Directly behind that was a field surrounded by thick woods on either side, a field about 40 meters across and maybe 200 meters long towards the bay. The field itself was definitely a cleared section of the woods with a lawn and definitely resembled the lead up to some sort of estate that would have been sitting at the back overlooking the bay. But again, no remnants of that estate remained, no stories of it either. Just a very manmade looking landscape in the middle of a wooded area that looked to have served some purpose at one time. It was very secluded being surrounded by the woods and the entry to it blocked by the memorial. It was rarely ever used and the woods on either side often contained dark weird items, bullet casings, lots of porn magazines that have been ripped up and pages blown through the woods, signs of encampments no longer used, etc. It was a desolate weird part of the park.

Back then people used to buy beer and go and sit in the park at night and drink. There wasn't much else to do, and beer, nor soda for that matter, still didn't come in aluminum cans all that often, it was mostly glass bottles.

Budweiser made these little glass bottles called "Nips" which were the most common bottles drank by people in this park, judging by what we would repeatedly find. Being only about 10 or 11 in 1981 we almost never saw anyone back there drinking because they went in there after dark, and even if we were out late, which often we were at that age, we still were cautious to enter the deeply wooded vast park after dark because it was very dark, and very scary. It wouldn't be for another year or two that we would run that park freely at night, but even then, it was always scary, both in a who is in here kind of way as well as a supernatural forces way. Something always felt off in that park at night.

But these were the days of litter and the thought of taking your trash with you was not a thing yet, so every morning afterward, there would be dozens and sometimes hundreds of these empty nips brown beer bottles laying around at different areas of the park, one of the most common was the memorial.

Cleaning up the park did not seem to be in the list of duties for the parks department at that time either, the park was for the most part very littered and one of the favorite pastimes for us was smashing bottles. So, we would walk into the park and see all the bottles at the memorial in the morning after, and proceed to throw the bottles, one at a time, for hours sometimes, at the memorial, smashing them into tiny little bits of glass, and throwing them harder and harder, and farther and farther. The different areas would become so covered in broken glass over the years that it would eventually break down and almost start to resemble sand. Keep in mind we were 9 and 10 years old at this time, a sense of decorum in our lives had not yet been taught to us or learned.

In 1979 the movie "the Warriors" came out, and it was

probably a year or two before someone got a bootleg copy on a Betamax or something and we watched it, at which point we declared ourselves a gang and cut vests out of t-shirts and got iron-on names on the back and started to patrol that park during the day, claiming it our "Turf". In 1983 we would have been 11 and 12 years old, and that was us, a gang of pre-teens hanging out in a park that was no good trying our hardest to be up to no good. We pseudo adopted the moniker "Dead End Kids" from the 1940's television show and by 1982 some of our destruction had already been written about in local newspapers. Stories written by upcoming reporters who undoubtedly thought they were describing a real street gang that scrawled their name on their turf but were instead writing about a bunch of 11 year old children that were largely unsupervised.

The violence associated with throwing a glass bottle against a concrete wall or monument as hard as you can is real. The sound alone is awe inducing. And imagine doing this repeatedly, 10, 20, 50 times in a session? Probably about 3 days a week?

There were piles of glass bottles left behind everywhere, multiple nights a week. Golden Field as it was known was the official park to the North of the parking lot and the Vietnam memorial and not to be confused with that open lawn in the wooded area. Golden Field was largely used for sports and housed three baseball diamonds and fields, so big that all baseball diamonds could be completely played and manned all the way to outfield at one time without any interference from the other fields. It was surrounded by a very picturesque, paved path that had a slight rolling hill. The path continued past the baseball fields, past one of those always locked bathroom facility buildings, to a path that was still paved but disappeared under the canopy of the woods and ran along the back high area "cliffs" overlooking the freeway and Little Neck Bay.

The Golden Field section of this park was the most well maintained, once you got past the memorial, for some reason, and I still suspect it was private funding from John Golden himself, there was not much litter, not much broken glass, only green grass and picturesque scenes. It also could be that this part of the park directly backed up on the richer neighborhood of houses to the north of mine and my friends, and we were already the richer neighborhood from the modest pocket of houses on the Southwest side of the park, so it seemed the quality of the park trickled up the closer to the bay and further North you got.

The more Southern park, Crocheron proper, didn't have many houses near it once you got deep inside, plus it was much larger, had much more heavy woods. It had a decent sized lake in the park separated from the bay by the freeway, and the lake had a very picturesque heavily wooded surround, with an access road that dead ended at the bottom. This was a lover's lane of sorts at the time and people would come down here and do nasty shit in their cars.

Once in a while when we would see a car parked and shaking with a couple inside, we would all rush the car and shake it violently and stand on the hood screaming as the couple inside tried to gather themselves in horror. That sounds like an innocent enough prank, but this was not long after the Son of Sam was killing lovers in their cars, and he did have a victim that he followed from our area. We didn't really understand this at the time but when I got older, I realized how bad the timing was and what kind of fear was in our communities back then.

Back towards Golden Field, still in the Crocheron side of the park there was one baseball diamond that backed up to the tennis courts fenced area separated by a paved path. This baseball diamond had a low brick wall across the path partially concealed by trees adjacent to the tennis courts. This brick wall was another popular place for people to sit and drink beers at night, and since this was the Crocheron side, it was not a vigorously upkept as the Golden side. This was one of our favorite places to smash bottles and throw them with ill intent against the low brick wall. There were inches of shattered glass ground to sand here from the years of doing this.

Perhaps the strangest thing is a lot of this happened in the areas just three or four feet off of the paved pathways that made their way through the park, the violence, the vandalism, the porn, and other yet to be discussed dark sides of society. Just hidden from view were newer, unofficial pathways beaten into the surrounding brush and wooded areas by constant travel of locals looking to make their own paths off the ones the park and city provided. Paths beaten into the woods long before we got there, I mean we got there in the later 1970's and they were already there, there was already vandalism, the bathroom buildings were already locked, there was already broken glass and bottles littered as far as we could see.

There were other things too the further away from the city provided and maintained areas you went, there were burnt out cars, empty husks of new and old automobiles, sometimes burned, sometimes stripped beyond recognition, some of them had been there when we got there and some became part of the landscape, trees growing through them.

When I talk about the violence implicit with the angry smashing of the bottles, that was not our violence, but violence we were led to as children walking these paths. The things we would find back there and the things we would participate in became rites of passage growing up in this part of NYC in the late 1970's, through the 1980's, into the 1990's. The world was different than it is now, it has almost nothing in common with today's world. You were not influenced by television, in the 1970's there was no television really, not like today. No social media, no influencers, no idols. Our idols were the legends in our neighborhoods that bucked the system and did the things we wanted to do. Our influences were the things we learned on these paths, the places they would lead us.

Our daily lives started off like the film Stand By Me, "you want to see a dead body?" ...of course we did.

You learn the most about yourself when you are put to the test outside of society. When you have to stand and defend yourself, when you have to face your fears with no one holding your hand. Our parents never really even asked what we did all day or how we got the black eye. Sometimes they did, but they didn't really care about the answers. They were fighting their own economic war, to keep a roof over our heads and food on our tables. There was no bank accounts, no investing. College was a pipedream in my neighborhood. It was hand to mouth, paycheck to paycheck, late on bills stress day in and day out for them. Stress pushed my father to smash a full coffee pot against the wall in our kitchen sending glass and hot coffee across all of us, this was our breakfast.

They did what they could with the 12% interest rates the bank would charge on home loans, there was no medical insurance. I think medical insurance started in the 1970s during Nixon, I think, from what I remember from my parents. I did not research back now, because it doesn't matter. This is the world we lived in.

THE MARINA

Gibson's dad worked a hot dog cart on the pier of the Marina, not clear to me looking back now if he owned that cart or just manned it as an employee of the Marina. He was missing an eye, or had a badly damaged eye, that was very cloudy white and sideways, also unclear if that was glass or the actual damaged eye still in place.

Kids used to refer to him as "The one eyed fish (Racist insults added)" but it never seemed to bother Gibson, but I guess it had to. I mean his closest friends like us would never say it but other kids in the neighborhood would. Gibson also started working down at the marina at a very young age. He was always very handy with tools and building and had a great work ethic altogether. He was a year older than us, and had a job down there always it seemed and by 14 years old was manning the little slip boat that would drive rich people out to their anchored boats and back to the pier and vice versa. A pretty cool job I always thought, and the marina was a great place to be.

The road from our neighborhood that led to it dead ended at the freeway to the North part of that wealthy area I mentioned adjacent to Golden Park. That was where the "Yacht Club" sat, an exclusive pool club and summer club for rich people that none of us were ever able to experience.

At least not legally, we did use all of the pool facilities at the yacht club on a daily basis, but on hot summer nights long after it closed for the day. An army of children would scale the fences, some of them barbed wired, and use the high dive facilities and pools and each morning they would return and find much of the patio furniture in the pool and it was part of their daily routine putting the place back together each day. I mean they called the police and occasionally they came with the police in the middle of the night and chased a swarm of 10 year olds out, and sometimes maybe even grabbed a kid or too, but what was the consequence? They brought them home talked to the parents and that was it. The kid would be back there the next day with the rest of us.

Eventually they just accepted it, it was our neighborhood, they existed in our world, not the other way around.

From that dead end street there was a wooden overpass set of stairs that went to an entirely wooden foot bridge over the freeway, that came down on the bay side at the marina. There were two of these such bridges. This one at the marina, and one about a mile further South connecting Crocheron Park directly over the freeway, with a picturesque walk up through a cobbled wall area and thick woods.

Get the idea? Our world centered around this park, which connected the areas where we lived to the areas we wished we lived, well kind of, we didn't really care about money yet, it was just our world.

The wooden bridges were something special too. Made entirely of wood that had been worn smooth as silk from ocean air and saltwater and heavy traffic for decades upon decades probably dating back to the 1920's. If you ran your hand along any part of it too fast you might catch an occasional splinter from an unworn spot, but for the most part it was worn to a glasslike finish, with paths of wear actually reducing the thickness of the wood in heavier use places.

The rails separating us from the cars below on the freeway were low too, just standard 36" rails. Decades later they would come add chain-link fences there about 6 feet high as is commonly seen on footbridges now, but not then. And to my knowledge, even with all of the insanity and kids climbing over the rails and walking holding on for dear life on the traffic side ledges, and playing, no one had ever fallen off into the speeding cars below.

"Ol' one eye!" was the more politically correct way to refer to Gibson's dad by some of the less abrasive kids in the neighborhood, as if there was such a thing as political correctness yet. There wasn't. But it was still said as a jab, not in any sort of endearing way, you know the drill, kids are inherently mean, I think.

Anton Nickolas was one of the worst offenders. He was the son of a trash collector, a seemingly good family, married mom and dad and a sister about a year younger than him. But he was really kind of crazy. He was one of us and with us always and he would start this sort of robotic voice that would over accentuate the beginnings of a phrase that kind of became a thing in the neighborhood. And every time he saw Gibson, he would call Gibson "OLLLLLLLLLLLLLL ONNNNEEEE EYED!!!!!! FISHHHHHHHHHHHHHHHHH...." It was very annoying and something Gibson pretty much became numb to; he didn't seem to care.

And remember consequences? Maybe more to this story later, maybe not, but when we got a little older, the paths that we followed would lead us to another rite of passage in our town, and that was to steal cars. And Anton Nickolas used to pick me up every day to drive me to school in a different stolen car, at least I suspected them mostly stolen. He eventually developed a very bad drug habit smoking crack which was gripping the nation at this time. And one day Anton would not show up, but another kid "Jason Maxima" would come to my house pounding on the door - "Put on the news!" He exclaimed.

Anton Nickolas had killed a girl the night before at a local bar a couple blocks away from my house driving a stolen car high on drugs and was in police custody. That was the last time any of us would see Anton Nickolas until he resurfaced from prison a decade later.

But let's get back to the hot dogs.

Gibson's dad's hot dogs were GOOD, most New York City hot dogs with the orange onions were great, "dirty water dogs" they called 'em. To this day when I go to New York I cannot wait to have one, but the hot dog carts of the day are now replaced with more ethnic cuisine carts that may be selling hot dogs, but not always the authentic ones with the right onions. They focus more on selling ethnic foods of the countries that the owners come from.

Just not the same hot dogs, so you got to search now for the right carts. Hot dog carts back then used to also have potato knishes, the square ones that would just be wrapped in foil and put in the under part of the burner to keep them hot, it wasn't intended for food to be warmed there, but they all did it. And a knish sliced with mustard and onions was one of the greatest things I have ever eaten to this day.

They also had a "Hot sausage" which was really just a fat hot dog but with a little spice, also amazing.

About a decade ago while in New York trying to find a knish at a cart I found out that mayor Bloomberg's office had outlawed the selling of the knishes because the carts weren't designed for that. I had several long conversations with different cart vendors about it and the good old days, and I had been eating them my entire life and no one I knew ever got sick from one.

Further down the pier from Gibson's dad's hot dog cart was a bait and tackle shop, people used to fish from the pier, and also a small café that served grilled foods like burgers and whatnot. Someplace we never ate because we never had any money.

Hot dogs at the cart were about 50c at the time and we knew Gibson's dad so occasionally we would get a hot dog, but that was about it, for the most part you ate at school lunch and then maybe a snack of some chips when you got out, but kids were generally pretty hungry all day long back then.

SCHOOL

There were two school options for kids that lived around the park. One was Sacred Heart, a Catholic school, that was relatively cheap but did cost some sort of monthly donation. Most of us went here. And there was PS 41, which was the public school and that was located at the Southwest corner of the park itself, right at the edge of the modest pocket of houses. My brother attended this school for some reason for a year before switching to the Catholic school. I always attended the Catholic school from 1st grade on, I also skipped kindergarten for some reason, they said it was aptitude related and I was tested for reading and math skills which were very high.

But skipping this grade made me young. I was already going to be starting six months younger than most kids because of my birthday, now they advanced me another year which meant I was 1 ½ years younger than the other students in my grade. Eventually I would start taking the train 2 hours to Bronx Science when I was 12 years old, and be scheduled to graduate high school not long after I turned 17. I wound up screwing up my senior year and did not graduate until I was 18 anyway but that was because of the graffiti. Good ol' graffiti.

Gibson attended PS 41. Trent, who will come up later, attended PS 41 in the beginning too before switching to Sacred Heart. Jimmy went to Sacred Heart, etc.

Thinking back, Catholic School in NYC in the 1970's? All nuns and priests; my brother approached me one day when all of the controversy was in the media in the 90's about the rampant sexual abuse, and he asked me, "You know, Sacred Heart? Nothing happened to us right? There's not something I'm suppressing here?"

We were altar boys; we were alone with the priests after school sometimes one on one and in small groups. We had a music teacher Mr. Ropak, a very heavy set, heavy breathing man that would lean over to help you play and teach us the Music as EGBDF "Every Goof Boy Deserves Fudge" when the rest of the world would teach it as "Every Good Boy Does Fine". What did he mean by Fudge?

Nothing, he meant nothing.

The answer is no, nothing happened. I mean the nuns were for sure physically abusive for discipline, and most of the Catholic priests had faces beet red from being drunk all day, but nothing was out of line in terms of abuse beyond that, nothing sexual at all. And we went for 8 years from 1975-1983.

Our experience always made me wonder about all of these claims because there were claims about the diocese where my school was and the priests were part of, but how could we have had an entire school that just was on the level when the entire Catholic school system was brought into question? Maybe we were just very lucky. Or maybe, just maybe, it was a witch hunt? I don't know. And believe me I have no loyalty to the Catholic church. In fact, the last time I was in a Catholic church would be in 1982 when I graduated from Sacred Heart.

When people would later ask my brother why he no longer was a practicing Catholic, he would reply "I guess I got choked with my own necktie once too often." He would hold a grudge. While we were in high school, Sacred Heart would continue to send the monthly donation envelopes to our house long after we grew out of the school. And my dad would keep making the donations because non practicing Catholics have this guilt that if they continue to donate to the church their soul will somehow be saved and that was the single soul saving activity my dad participated in.

But my brother found out he was still sending them money so he started intercepting the envelopes from the mail before my dad would get home and throwing them away, eliminating the donations and my dad never even wondered why they stopped asking him.

We sometimes walked to school, most kids did, and we walked home sometimes too but often my mom used to go to great lengths to always try to leave work and pick us up and drop us off. She had this parental fear that we would wind up on the side of a milk carton or something. It seemed "Kidnapping" was on everyone's mind. And it was not a long walk, but something my mom just always wanted to do.

From my house directly across the street in the Park, there was a large field and at the back end of that field was a beaten path in the grass down to raw dirt that would travel through a small wooded area, down a valley and back up the other side between two other, not yet mentioned, baseball diamonds. These were smaller baseball diamonds, often used for little league and tee ball. Once you came up on the south side of the park, the modest section of houses was immediately to the right, and to the left was an Irish Catholic pocket, names like McKernan, Costigan, were common.

Straight up two blocks you make a left and two more blocks you would see a red brick church and surrounding buildings, gothic inspired, with a newer portion, and this was Sacred Heart church and school.

When we arrived in the morning there was a sea of children running quite literally amok on the side yard of the school, not fenced in. It is a large grassy area that has had the grass stomped into oblivion by angry little feet over the years and the entire center, 90% of the grassy field was basically a dirt lot. On dry warmer days there would be a cloud of dust hovering amongst the children.

At Sacred Heart you had to wear a school uniform. The girls were in a little pleated blueish green plaid skirt about knee length, knee high socks and a light blue or yellow (They get to choose!) button up shirt. There was a little vest that would go over the shirt if they wanted.

The boys would wear grey pants with a light blue shirt, or yellow, but in the boys case it was almost always light blue, I think I only remember 2 yellow shirts amongst the boys in 8 years. And if a boy was in a yellow shirt it was confusing, like did he work for the school or something?

The boys would also wear plaid neckties that matched the girls' skirts and vests. Most kids wore real ties but some like my brother started wearing clip on ties as a defense mechanism. I always hated clip on ties, they were just so fake. And there was something satisfying to tying your own tie and working on the knot to get it to look right.

Sometimes when you were particularly out of line, the nuns would pin you against the wall and sinch your tie very tight around your neck choking you as they muttered some threats of bad behavior through gritted teeth.

When they let go you would quickly reach to loosen it, it was really dangerous in retrospect, but once in a while they would go after a kid with a clip on tie and not realizing it is a clip on, they would go to yank it tight only to have the tie come off in their hands to the laughter of the children which would make them even madder.

In that front school yard there was a brick wall that surrounded the garbage dumpsters on the side yard to conceal them from view of the neighbors. The wall started at 2 feet tall and because of the slope of the ground it got taller and taller before making its return to the building. By the end of the wall it was almost 8 feet high. And kids used to walk out to the high part and starting there would sit on the wall, all the way down to the low part, and other kids used to run up when kids weren't looking and jump and push kids off the wall. Amazing no one was ever killed as it was concrete below, and almost no one was ever really even hurt, no one seemed to care, not the kids, and especially not the nuns who didn't care until that bell rang.

And when that bell rang, it was a Little House on the Prairie type thing, a handheld bell that looked like it was a holdover from the revolutionary war. A heavy brass bell about 12" tall with a worn wooden handle about 12" long above it. Something Paul Revere might have been ringing when the British were coming. And some nun or a student that day who was chosen would stand there and throw their body into ringing it up and down, at which time a hush would slowly fall over the kids playing, bell ringing the whole time until the kids all fell into lined formation awaiting entry into the school.

There were other pranks that took place in that school-yard every morning, deadly ones. Kids used to crawl up behind other kids while a kid in front would push the kid standing over the kid that secretly crawled up behind them. This could have been deadly for a number of reasons and did result in a fractured wrist one day.

Another popular move happened to a good friend of ours Kenny. He was standing on a chilly morning with his hands in his front pockets and Eric snuck up behind him simultaneously grabbing the cuffs of each pant leg and yanking them as hard as he could. Kenny immediately left his feet being sent smashing forward into the

40

ground. This was done all of the time and usually a kid gets his arms out in front of him and it's not too bad. But Kenny had his hands in his pockets, and well, he could not get them out in time. He landed face first on the concrete and was a bloody mess.

No police were called, no one was suspended, Kenny was iced up and went home for the day and would return the next day looking like a truck smashed him in the face, but life went on.

FORT TOTTEN

I briefly mentioned this before but there's so much more to say. In 1981 there were two brothers that lived a few blocks over from us and down the block from one of our best friends, they were about 2 or 3 years older than us.

We found out they were selling a 1979 Honda 50cc dirt bike and we asked our dad if he could get it for us. Not entirely sure what my dad was thinking when he said yes. Probably he was thinking it would stop us from bugging him and give us something to do. We lived within the New York City limits and those bikes were and still are illegal to ride within the limits and never mind the fact that we were children.

"You just going to ride it in the park?" He said, talking about the city park "Crocheron" that was across the street from us. Looking back, that itself was insane, thinking it was ok to send your children into the city park on an illegal dirt bike unsupervised while you are at work. "Yes!" we said, because what else were we going to say?

"Stay off the streets!" he exclaimed as he put us in his Cadillac to drive the few blocks to pick up the bike. It cost him $150 which I guess was a decent amount of money at the time but wasn't really all that much either.

I mention my dad's Cadillac often, it, and several others over the years, were his pride and joy, his one treat. He had a connection to a car dealer that got him deals too good to be true. The guy would eventually be indicted for tax evasion, my dad was surprised, but as an italian-american family we all knew what was up. But my dad? He was in denial supposedly.

When someone would put a bomb under his Cadillac El Dorado in our driveway at the end of the 80s, the media showed up and couldn't wait to out him and his friend as mobsters, even though the bomb was intended for his kids. And especially insulting since my dad worked twelve hour days six days a week.

Craziest thing about the dirt bike is, as I mentioned, there was no helmet, the thought never even came up. He bought us a gasoline powered dirt bike and did not buy us a helmet. But safety wasn't really something people were all that conscious of at that time. I mean you could pick up seven kids in your Cadillac, all without seat belts and get on the highway and wave to a cop and he would wave back. It was mostly lawless at that time.

The bike was clutch-less and had two gears, both down from neutral at the top (If you ride motorcycles, you know what that means if not it references the gearing pattern on the left foot shifter), it was easy enough to ride and my dad watched as his two children got on, me driving with my brother on the back and disappeared into the park across the street.

The park, as I've described, was heavily wooded and had many fields and connecting parks and areas all inside one massive park that backed right up to the Cross Island Parkway right against Little Neck Bay, from the park we could get on the foot bridge made of wood with the mini bike because it was small and ride it down some long low rise steps on the bay service road which would then give us access to Northern Blvd if we went to the right and The Marina and then Fort Totten if we went left, all along a separated service road by the highway. This service road was for official vehicles and people bringing boats to the marina only for the most part and was occasionally patrolled by the military police from Fort Totten which sat in the shadow of the Throgs Neck Bridge across the bay from The Bronx, on the Queens side.

Until this day I don't think my father had any idea how far our access through that park went for us on the minibike or that we were across the highway by the bay riding 3 miles down by an amazing old civil war military base from 1862. I think Fort Totten is still available to tour, at the time we were children it was still in use somewhat and there were military there, not sure what its current status is.

What my dad did not want also happened, we turned the front yard of our house and part of our neighbor's yard into a dirt bike trail complete with jumps and a worn path in the grass. He was furious but he would see us, and a bunch of the neighborhood kids riding on it and did not have any options besides to smile and just go into the house at that point, the damage was done while he was at work and he knew it would happen again, he knew us.

The little minibike topped out at about 30mph in 2nd gear which for a young child with no helmet was quite a high speed, amazing that we never really got injured on it either.

For the next year we would be menaces to that park and the road along the bay and nobody would really have anything to say about it. During baseball games, players and fans would watch us buzz along the edges of the outfield as we went by. Mostly to waves of support from moms of the older kids and the occasional yell of "Get off the field!"

There was a long-gone kid from my neighborhood that I was friends with named Bobby Raz who had experience with dirt bikes on account of his older brothers. He had a hearing impairment and wore hearing aids and was a tough kid, always fighting would-be bullies one on one in the neighborhood for making fun of him.

Unfortunately, this friend of mine wouldn't make it to 18 years old without developing a serious addiction problem and going on to be a mess into adulthood. He credits an incident that happened with me and him on the dirt bike as traumatizing him. I am not sure if that incident really did put him over the edge, but this is what happened.

He and I set out one day on the dirt bike with me driving, we were eleven years old at the time and we made our way through the park, across the bridge and down the service road toward Fort Totten as we had done many times before. Once you pass the marina on the right there is a densely wooded area that backs into the military base, this area has some beaten paths in it, but it was generally not traveled by anyone except vagrants or people looking to go fuck in the woods or do drugs, that kind of thing.

We passed the marina and started out on one of these paths away from the road when there were two men blocking our path, they looked like the typical white dirtbags of the day with long mullets, jeans and dirty clothes on, probably junkies or something. They told us to stop, told us they were police but as we got closer we could clearly see that they weren't police so we turned to ride off as one of them tried to grab Bobby and at this point they were cursing at us, saying things like "Get the fuck over here!" Bobby broke free and we started to ride away but the path was very rough making it difficult to ride and we were barely outpacing them, as we got back towards the service road they had a beige piece of shit car there and they jumped in and chased us onto the service road.

Our minibike only had a max speed of 30 mph, which as I said is fast for a kid, but it's not fast compared to a car. It wasn't long before they ran us off the road and grabbed us and were trying to stuff us into the back of their car with us hysterically crying and screaming and kicking.

There was no one around to help us until two military

women, who happened to be jogging along the service road, saw what was happening. They ran over and started screaming for help until one of the dirtbags tried to say he was a cop busting us for the minibike.

"Let me see your badge!" The woman, now holding my arm, screamed at the guy at the top of her lungs.

He flashed something in his wallet, and she was not believing him. "Go get help!" She screams to the other woman as the one that stayed behind starts pulling us away from the dirtbags, they threaten her but quickly think better of the "Help" this other woman ran off to get and they jump in their car and speed off.

The woman walks us back to the service road and we wait until the other woman pulls up in the back of a government sedan with two military police officers.

They explain to the MPs what happened, and these two soldiers help us out. The first guy goes back into the woods and retrieves our dirt bike while the other one radios for the police.

A police car from the 109th precinct pulls up, and of course no one cares that we are illegally riding the dirt bike anymore because here you have two young children that were the victims of predators, and an attempted abduction. The cops take over, the ladies hug us and head on their way.

The cop tries to put my dirt bike in the trunk of the car but it will not fit. He tells me to ride it home and he will follow right behind me with Bobby in the car and his emergency squad car lights for safety.

We cannot go over the bridge because obviously the cop car couldn't drive over a narrow wooden footbridge, so they tell me to go out onto Bell Blvd and ride that main street all the way up past Bay Terrace and towards my house, which I do.

That ride was one of the coolest memories of my childhood, despite the awful events of the day. Many kids from the neighborhood saw me in what they thought was a police chase and were cheering me as I passed them.

When we got back, they dropped Bobby off to his dad and then waited with me for my parents to get home from work about an hour later. They explained what happened and wanted us to come down to the station and talk to a sketch artist, said the women would also be doing that and that they wanted to show us some photos of known predators in the area as well.

Bobby's parents didn't want to go.

My mom screamed "I knew it" when she learned of our attempted abduction, she had always feared this, and now coincidentally it came true.

We went down to the station, drew up a couple of sketches and looked though a few books of pictures but none looked like the guys.

They never did make an arrest and to this day I wonder what was their intent had they gotten us?

Being a kid at the time I always assumed it was for ransom because that's the kid way of thinking. As an adult now looking back, I am sure it was something far more nefarious.

Chapter 2

HOW TO HOP A TURNSTILE (Part I)

What do you do as a New York City Kid in the 1980s
with almost no money in your pocket when your night
and day consists of constantly getting on and off the
subway train? Keep in mind, there were only tokens
available at this time, there were no unlimited ride metro cards, or any metro cards at all. It was a brass token
that looked much like a quarter and had an NYC logo
in the center, sometimes punched out, sometimes not,
there were several iterations over the years.

When I was just about 13 years old I started commuting to Bronx Science daily from Queens, up until that
point I was only on the subway with my Uncle, or rarely
on a day we ditched school when I was about 11. You
would get a transit pass that, from what I remember was
a green card. We would carry that and show the guy in
the token booth and they would buzz the exit gate, or
sometimes the exit gate didn't even lock and you would
pull it open and show this card from a distance. He never asked to see it up close because if you ignored him, he
was never going to come out of that booth if he was the
only one in the station.

The glass to the token booth was bulletproof and he was
pretty much safe in there from the evils of the world and
the evils of NYC in the 1970s and 1980s, much of which
wound up down in the subway at one point or another.

There was a way the token clerk could get got in there
though, because like most things evil, humanity has a

way of figuring out how to be as fucking rotten to one another as possible, in this case some awful people figured out that if someone took a lighter fluid refill or a charcoal igniting fluid squeezable container, they could squeeze the fluid in through that little money cut out at the bottom of the glass onto the guy in the booth and light him on fire.

It sounds disgusting to even type that and it was something I had witnessed the aftermath of one time in my life and was something that I, nor anyone I was ever with had participated in. I wouldn't stand for such a thing even as a child. But this was our world, the world Travis Bickel loathed and lamented in Taxi Driver, the world where in Times Square there was no innocence for kids our age and explicit sexual posters and theaters lined every street complete with pimps, prostitutes, drug dealers and scumbags end to end as far as the eye could see in any direction.

Even outside of Times square I remember one theater on the corner of 14th street and maybe 2nd Ave. advertised in huge letters and accompanying images "All Male Chinese" for almost two decades all the way into the 1990s. And while there may be nothing wrong with "All Male Chinese" being your thing, it was weird for children like us to see when we were never told or learned about anything of that sort except on the streets.

It was normal for us to find hardcore porn magazines in alleyways and parks back then, sometimes even stacks of hardcore photo prints discarded or thrown all over an alleyway. This was long before the days of the internet and porn being easily accessible, for the most part to watch porn at this time adults, or teens, had to go to an adult theater or peep show booth or buy hardcopies and take it someplace. I mean think about this for a minute, those theaters and peep show booths, guys were watching porn in there, what do guys do when watching porn? Yeah, they had the mops and buckets ready.

Or perverts took hard copies to a hidden place that was public. Much of it was cringeworthy, some of it we started to find in hidden areas in the city and parks as early as 8 or 9 Years old. Which brings up another thing.

We were latch key kids, I think that's what they called us, both parents at work until 6 or 7 every day, no one there to pick us up from school. I mean my mom did pick me up many days and then drop me off before going back to work because she was scared for me but some days we just walked. We sometimes wore a key around our necks and walked home from school in groups sometimes when we were just 8 years old as long as some of us were 9 or 10.

The first time I got "Grabbed" for anything I was 8 years old, it was snowing out and I was in a snowsuit and walking with a group of kids near Bay Terrace Gables, an exclusive enclave of wealthy homes. One of the 11 year olds in the group threw an icy snowball at a house and it broke the window, the owner came charging out and kids scattered everywhere. Me being in a snowsuit made me very slow, I looked like a teddy bear and the owner grabbed me dragging me back towards his house. The 11 year old kid that threw the snowball was a good friend of ours named Richie B. He did the right thing and immediately ran back when he saw I got caught and talked to the owner and had them call his mom to arrange to pay to fix it and then Richie brought me back home.

But crazy, it was kids raising other kids.

After school many times we didn't even go home and stayed out in the neighborhood, usually with other kids, sadly sometimes alone, until the street lights came on and we knew our parents would be home soon. Today my son is 9 and is kept locked in the school until an adult (Or I think they will accept a known teenager) shows up for him, what a difference, I couldn't imagine my little kid on the streets the way we were.

But all of that is neither here nor there when it comes to hopping turnstiles is it? It's related to the quality of life in this city of ours at the time though. The city averaged 1500-2000 murders per year at this time and probably about 20,000 almost fatal assaults per year, maybe more. In light of what could have happened to you, hopping turnstiles was a simple way of life crime that was as necessary as it was satisfying.

The school pass wouldn't always work late after school hours, sometimes they wouldn't open the gate for you, and many times we just simply did not have it on us. I kept mine in my bookbag which meant coming to and from school and hanging out immediately afterward I would have it on me, but most of the times I found myself roaming the city I would not. It had my name on it, you didn't bring anything with your name on it when you went out to cause havoc in the subway system. There was no carrying I.D. at this time.

And as I got older some of my friends were out of school already and never had passes to begin with so hopping was the way to go.

"Fare evasion" was the official name of the crime given by the law and if you got caught you could potentially face arrest but most of the times it was a ticket, sometimes both. Prior to being 16 it usually resulted in a telephone call to your parents and then the cops would cut you loose.

The optics of "fare evasion" varied, in some instances writers would have robbed conductors or station workers, or simply ran off with their stuff finding their keys inside. On their keyrings they had keys to master locks of the subway system which included padlocks on gates at closed down or unmanned exits from stations, depending on who we were with, they would sometimes open these gates and you would go inside the station.

Other stations had little tricks, ways you could climb up onto the backside of the station platform and shimmy out into the system undetected, one trick in particular was on the RR line at 8th street, or was it Astor? in the Village. This is a trick we used all of the time when we went to skate the Brooklyn banks and were 13 and 14 years old, the time this worked best because we were still small. On Broadway at the exit only part of the station the gate had a full height exit turnstile at one side with a locked gate at the other. The top of the gate and turnstile in this spot came to about 9" from the ceiling, not much space but just enough that if you weren't really huge you could climb up and squeeze thru, throwing whatever you were carrying over before you went. We did this one often, and you got to know these little things at different parts of the city as needed.

There was also the common method of waiting until you hear the train pulling into the station just out of view of the token booth clerk, then like a baseball fury, running out and literally "Hopping" the turnstile and running down (or up) to get on the train that was just pulling in. As you did this method the token clerk would always yell on the loudspeaker for the Police and says things Like "The police are already waiting downstairs" or other things to scare you, but he knew damned well they weren't going to delay the train in the station waiting for police just for a couple of kids.

Of course, sometimes there were cops on the train or in the station and they would be notified and that's just bad luck, that would end with us running into the tunnel in which case uniform cops would never pursue in there. Or if they got the jump on you it would result in apprehension. It was common for city kids to get grabbed by the cops for any number of things on a regular basis, this being one of them.

One time, Cro RIS and I were bombing Grant Ave. lay-up in Brooklyn, I want to say it was very early 1986, I was 15 at the time, and we used to go to that lay-up via a city bus that would drop us off in the neighborhood. I should add that the neighborhood locals weren't exactly friendly around there to people coming into their neighborhood to commit crimes and there have been many instances of things getting crazy with the locals in fights with Gato, Neo and others, something me and Cro hoped to avoid.

Often when traveling to lay-ups in certain neighborhoods, we took city buses instead of the train because people or police seeing you get off the train at certain stations with bags, especially at odd hours led to immediate suspicion that you were a graffiti writer, and that was never something you wanted on your way into a lay-up.

The Grant Ave. station platform was in relatively close proximity to the back of the trains parked in the lay-up and was generally a pretty hot station with both writers and/or cops so after getting off the city bus we would not go through the station. We would walk the street along the subway line and enter the tracks by climbing over or thru the fence between the last elevated station and where it descends into the tunnels toward the Pitkin Yard, then hiding until the train passed and running into the descending tunnel directly behind the last car.

This was a common practice when it came to entering tunnels, especially if there might be a bit of a longer walk, you always had to worry about the train coming in behind you and trapping you in one of those low clearance areas and killing you or spotting you and calling the police etc. Funny thing was, once in a while, someone would be looking out the back window and see you run in behind the train and get excited or surprised but looking out the back of the train was usually done by kids or loners or writers, so it wasn't really a cause to end the day.

Entering Grant this way meant you had to look for the ladder, which in my time was marked with a QUIK RTW tag, that descended to the parked trains one level below from the tunnel we were currently in.

Once below, at the front of these three or four parked trains (One or possibly two A trains, and Two CC trains or vice versa) you could see the station about 100 yards away. You had to be careful to not walk behind the trains on this side, this was true for many lay-ups, because the trains had the red and white safety lights on when parked in the tunnel.

If you walked around this end of the train and in front of the lights, it would appear to flicker if someone on the station was looking into the dark tunnel they might see this and know someone was in there. Also, after a couple hours of painting fumes from the paint make their way into the stations which already arose suspicion. This was especially a problem when painting outsides at lay-ups like Kingston on the number lines. The in-service train would speed past the lay-up and the draft would push all of the air and paint fumes into the station.

On this particular day we went back out the way we came in, no paint cans left on us, but we were covered in paint and filth. Cro and I walked to the next elevated station to take the train home connecting somewhere along the way to a train that goes to Flushing or Jamaica. We walked up the stairs and heard the train pulling in and ran and hopped the turnstile with the token clerk screaming for the Police as usual. We walked up the stairs toward the platform and Cro looked back past me then took off running fast jumping onto the tracks. I turned to see what he saw, and it was too late, the cop grabbed me by my jacket and threw me into the wall.

Cro had long-ish hair at the time and the first thing the cop says to me is "Where'd your girl go?" having only seen his hair from behind. "I don't know any girl" I said, as they roughly frisked me throwing everything in my army jacket pockets onto the floor. Oddly enough they didn't even mention all the caps or paint all over me, I think they thought I was homeless because I was so filthy, they may not have even associated me with the lay-up a few stations away because it was on another line and underground, exactly the reason we avoided using the lay-up stations.

They asked if I had parents, where I lived and if I went to school.

"Bronx Science" I told them, which they did not believe. One of them even mocked me "Yeah right!" he said. This was a common theme when the police asked me where I went to school. Bronx Science was prestigious, it was hard for people to believe that a street kid doing stupid shit went there.

They asked me for my phone number and walked me over to a pay phone and called my parents, he asked my mom what I looked like and if I went to Bronx Science, into the phone he said "Ok, keep him home next time, he's out here causing trouble and not paying his subway fares."

They let me go, back then we had no cell phones or any means to reach one another so I didn't catch up with Cro until another day back in Flushing.

Later in 1986 Cro took me to start hanging out with

Chino and his crew, hopping turnstiles became even more common with the group of about 20 of us all being from different boroughs and areas and then invading stations with 10-20 fare evaders at one time was something that they might delay a train for.

I had seen Chino up and knew of his crew but hadn't met him yet in 1986. Cro was at 175th lay-up with Chino and CAC and he came by Dot's house after he got back. Dot was a punk rock girl named Debby that was really close with the well-known graffiti writer (who we will call) Angel, and since I was almost always with Angel at the time I was often at Dot's. She had a separate entrance to her parent's house and her door was right near her basement room, so she could have people coming and going without her parents even knowing for the most part.

It was like 2am and Angel, Dot, and myself were sitting on Dot's bed when Cro showed up and told us a bit about the night, he told us Chino was walking with a fire extinguisher over his head ready to smash someone when they walked down a dark part of the tunnel entering the lay-up which was hotly contested with the local crew XX and other writers coming in. 175th Lay-up is a story in itself and we will for sure talk about that later.

Dot was an attractive punk rock girl, there was something about that look at the time, she had a shaved head with a little piece of a mohawk left and wore short kilt skirts with black tights and doc marten boots and always had lipstick on. We would sit on her bed often and get high, that's where I tried the drug, "Rush" for the first time. It was some sort of cleaning fluid that had an extremely noxious odor and if you inhaled it deeply your head would get this enormous rush to the point that it quite literally felt like it was 6 feet across, and I would lose spatial relevance and start spinning. One time doing it laying on her bed it felt like my head went right through her bedroom wall. Looking back, those types of drugs were probably the worst thing for us. God only knows what it did to our bodies to cause that effect.

On occasion the writer Mirage would stop by Dot's house too, he was good friends with Angel at the time. He already had a car, so I am assuming he was about 2 years older than me.

One time he pulled up and showed us some shirts he had been working on with the feet throw ups, they were pretty cool, light blue with puffy printed feet, not sure why I remember the shirts or him showing them to us so vividly but I do.

He had a different outlook on graffiti and would some-times in the daylight think it was ok to draw his feet on a city gate like it was legal, and I think he got away with that because at the time he was one of the first artists painting an icon instead of a name, in this case cartoon feet. People saw what he was writing and chose to not feel the same way they would if someone scribbled their name.

He passed away about a year after that unfortunately, an amazing artist gone way too soon.

At the end of one night at Dot's room, I asked Cro to take me with him the next time he went to bomb with

Chino and that's how Chino and I met, we all just went to hang out and cause trouble and run around Manhattan taking tags, mostly with markers.

That particular night we met Chino at his apartments in Fort Greene part of Brooklyn, there were about 15 writers already there, from TFK-TAX, FTS, KHB, and BYI. After congregating in the courtyard of the buildings for about half an hour we set out and down into an underground station. Chino walked over to the token booth and called out, "Hey, I need a police officer sir, please help, is there a police officer in the station?"

"No" replied the guy in the booth as the sound of the train coming in could be heard.

At that moment all 20 of us descended and hopped the turnstiles with the guy screaming on the PA, there were indeed cops on that train but it was not long after rush hour, the station was pretty busy and we all split up with about 2 or 3 of us jumping on every car, they delayed the train for a minute while the cops walked thru but they had no way to know exactly who was who on the packed train, and we all were pretending we had been there since before the station, so the train eventually pulled out and we made our way into "Money Makin'" (Manhattan).

BUS FARE EVADING - Wanna go for a ride? (Part II)

I've often told people that you cannot evade a bus fare but that is not true, there were several ways to do this.

At packed bus stops and with crowded busses sometimes kids would push the back door for you or you could squeeze in the back door while the bus was loading and unloading. The bus driver might catch you and push you off the bus, but I've done it, kids do it.

Another, way more interesting way and a way more dangerous way is going for a ride on the back of the bus which sometimes would lead to the top of the bus for the more risk inclined.

Busses in the later 80s in New York started to be modernized and the back window was covered by louvers that would vent the engine, they had slightly rounded bumpers which weren't great to stand on but if you grabbed the louvers you could hold on and get enough leverage from your feet to take the bus for a long way. Cars driving behind would often beep or scream or just fall back out of fear that you were going to fall off and they would run you over.

People on the sidewalk that watch you fly by at 40 miles per hour often cheered or laughed, and I assure you, no matter how many times you do this, when that bus gets up over 30 miles per hour, fear washes over you. It is an extreme sport type of adrenaline but fear none the less.

Sometimes kids would even muscle their way on top of the bus but once up there it was difficult to hold on to anything beside a small vent, so that was much less likely for most, I have never ridden the top of a bus.

We used ride the back often though, from the Q13 stop near 35th Ave. down to Bay Terrace, it was only about a mile but when that bus got hitting those bumps, every time, the noise, the exhaust, I always thought to myself "I'm never doing this again."

But like most adrenaline-fueled habits for a teenager, again would be very soon after because it was just too much fun.

MORRIS PARK – Esplanade (Part III)

In early 1986 "Done FPV" was working at an accessories store of some kind on Main Street in Flushing Queens, I have not had any contact with him since about the end of that year or have any idea what became of him, but at this time we used to meet up at his job when they closed at around 10pm and then head out. Both of us in army jackets, and both with 4 cans in the sleeves; usually our missions involved trying to hit different lay-ups that we had heard about but had not yet been to with anyone.

We mostly had no idea how to get in or had only heard stories on how, places like 175th, Esplanade, City Hall, etc. Usually, they were highly contested lay-ups and we showed up as two 15 and 16 year olds that were clueless. Sometimes the night ended in disaster, but most of the times in just disappointment with very little painting getting done for one reason or another.

His job was right next to the pizzeria that was on Main Street one short block towards Kissena Blvd. and directly across from Woolworth. The pizza was really good there, it wasn't Gloria's which was another block up on Roosevelt Ave and I believe is still there till this day, also great pizza.

When I would get off the Q13 bus at the intersection of Main Street and Roosevelt I could immediately see his job, brightly lit in fluorescent lighting with display tables out front and I would walk over and wait for him to get off. On this night we were going to head to Esplanade, specifically the stick outs by the tunnel. I had seen them before and heard about them but never bombed them.

By the cusp of 1987, I would successfully hit them and piece them a couple of times but that was with experienced writers, but for now we were showing up cold after a sixty minute train ride at 11:45 pm. We got off the train about three stops short of where the lay-up was and then we would walk and climb up one of the overpasses closer to the Morris Park Station. As I mentioned before, it was a bad idea to actually get off at the station/s where the trains were parked.

We found the spot, climbed up and were on the tracks, the trains were parked both directions from where we were standing, and the lights were on inside the trains for some reason. This immediately made us uneasy because most of the time when trains were laid up, they would be parked with the lights off. We did a quick throw up each before hearing and seeing people down the tracks and deciding "Fuck this" let's just get out of here. We climbed back down the little hill to the street and walked to the Morris Park station which I had never entered from the street before.

It was completely covered in graffiti and completely deserted, it was now about 2am or so. The station also had no one in the token booth and the gates were open to the platform access. I thought to myself "what in the dystopian hell is this?" where is everyone? Is the train free here?

We walked onto the platform, the lay-up trains were there in the station too and everything was deserted. We looked and could see the train approaching so we stood there as it pulled in. We were at one of the ends, thinking back now I don't know if it were the back or the front, but I do know not all of the doors opened. And the doors that did open had a cop step out and look both ways, we walked towards that door and there was a makeshift token collection system where we gave them a token right then and there to get on the train and we entered past the conductor manning the machine and the cop standing next to him, with the cop glaring at us as one of our cans rattled in our sleeves.

Honestly, I have never asked anyone about this since then and now almost 40 years later it feels like it was a strange dream, and maybe it was, maybe it was all a dream.

I mean, a cop collecting tokens in the middle of the night on the NYC Subway train?

Chapter 3

FIVE POINTS

Five Points was a large industrial building in Long Island City that was visible from the 7 line train as it made its final bend in Queens before going underground and then into Manhattan. Because of the visibility from the transit system, this building and particularly the rooftops, have long been a sought-after target for graffiti writers.

By the late 1990s it would become known as Five Points and be a legal graffiti spot for artists to go and paint at any time of the day without fear of other writers or police. Obviously sometimes other writers would show up and cause trouble, but for the most part it was a community place to paint for street artists from around the world that had visibility and connection to authentic New York City graffiti history and the train system.

Before it was Five Points however, it was called "Phun Phactory" or something like that in the earlier 90s. Also the same concept but not as organized yet.

But in the 1980s this industrial building was in use doing industrial shit, and it was completely illegal to go anywhere near it or climb on the roof or write on it. It was extremely dark and on a junkyard-esque dead end street under the elevated 7 train tracks and was private property. It was no more legal to climb on the roof and write there than it would be for someone to climb on the roof of your house and write graffiti.

But, as I said, rooftops along the 7 line, and most elevat-ed train lines were highly desirable for their exposure and graffiti writers would risk life and limb to hit them. Over the years several have died being chased and fall-ing to their deaths or shot by someone thinking a writer was a burglar.

There was a bar on the corner under the same elevated tracks that would be populated with local workers at night long after the industrial buildings of the area were closed for the day. I think that bar might still be there or at least it was until not that long ago.

In late 1985 we set out on that exact mission in the middle of the night, to hit that rooftop on that build-ing seven years before it would become a legal place to paint, and it went kind of wrong for us. But nothing that we can't look back at laugh at today, right?

It was myself, Nim, Tame, Taro, Jere and Nark DMS, we were all 14 and 15 years old with exception of Nim who I think just turned 16 a month or so prior.

We took the train to the elevated station above the bar, Court Sq. I think is what the station was called then. The tracks were very high here, much higher than many elevated trains as coming from Queensboro Plaza they went over a new series of, still under construction, elevated roadways connecting the Long Island Express-way to Roosevelt Island I think as well as additional approaches to the Queensboro Bridge.

We walked down the stairs to the street level and passed the bar, into the dark end of the block where the closed down industrial buildings were located. We looked for a way up and found some trash piled up against a broken down fence and a tree, it was wood pallets and other hard items we could climb on. Using a combination of that trash and the fence and the tree, we were able to gain access to the enormous roof. It was like three football fields in size from what I remember. We walked in towards the side of the building visible from the train. It was close to the train at this back side of the building but not so close that you really had to hide when the train passed, not at night.

The train did look really cool going by though, it was a very New York feeling to watch an elevated train go down the dark tracks at night with the interior lights on, seeing the New Yorkers being moved from one place to another. One of my fondest memories of growing up in New York.

We painted our pieces, Taro for some reason painted a big T and wrote Terminator in it. He had previously hooked up with Sin RIS and some CAC writers in Jamaica and because he was a talented artist he felt it would be embarrassing to be seen up with us toys. I say that joking but that is really why he painted the terminator T and not his tag.

When we were done, we went to climb down and were making a bit of a racket, too much noise and laughing

At this time some of the people from the bar were letting out and walking back to their cars parked in the dark parking lot of the building in the junkyard-esque area. They looked back when they heard us and assumed we were robbers or something and screamed "Hey Stop!"

We jumped down the rest of the way in a panic and took off running with them chasing us. Being young at the time it made sense to us to run back up the way we came and we climbed all of the steps at the elevated 7 station again and hopped the turnstile with these guys still chasing us. In a panic we ran out onto the tracks towards Queensboro Plaza.

Because we were all in school at the time, we went on these missions on weekends, it was now about 1am on a Friday night and these stations, especially Queensboro were kind of crowded. Plus the elevated tracks were so much higher than any tracks we had ever been on. Climbing down wasn't really an option, I don't even think we knew how to yet.

These guys did not come on the tracks after us but were gathered at the end of the platform screaming at us. We continued to walk towards the Queensboro Plaza station which was a bit of a hike. The train on the opposite track also heading towards Queensboro has arrived and is currently leaving the station we just left, the conductor sees us and stops his train, radioing in.

It was one of those classic, you know you are busted and going down in flames things. We started emptying our pockets, throwing anything we had, any cans left, caps, stickers etc. off the tracks to the street below. The cans were landing with a smash.

As we approached the Queensboro Platform the train

was there now on our side too, people on the platform were looking at us, and in the front of the train were three uniform police officers. We just stopped and stood there, in between stations with no place to go.

The train slowly moved towards us, the front door of the train now open, it stopped about 10 yards before us.

"Don't be stupid, just come to the train!" yelled one of the cops at our group of 15 year olds.

What choice did we have? We walked up and they helped us on the train which was packed now in the front car with onlookers on a Friday night. Laughing at us and clapping when the cop pulled the last one of us up.

The train stopped at the next station, the guys were still waiting for us, they told the cops we were trying to break into their building.

The cops frisked us and cuffed us and walked us down the stairs to the street below where there were two Transit Police Suburbans waiting for us.

I remember it like it was yesterday, as they loaded us in the cop on the radio looked back at us and shrugged as he said – "

"I've got 6, I dunno, bad-guys, in transit now." He was obviously at a loss of what to call us because were still children for the most part.

Back at the police station we told them exactly what we

were doing, they lambasted us and called our parents, we got tickets for trespassing on the tracks which was only a violation.

One by one our parents came to get us. Tame who was staying with us at the time had to be picked up by my dad as well.

Tame looked at my dad with shame in his eyes when we got in the car and said "You can hit me if you want."

Obviously, my dad did not hit him, but that sentiment from a house guest is hilarious, in some ways it must have been even more embarrassing to be picked up by someone else's father after being arrested.

It would be another few years before we would hit that spot again, and then eventually returning again in the early 2000s when it was Five Points to paint one day for old times' sake.

Chapter 4

GONE RACKING

There was a term that was used when I was growing up which meant to get needed supplies for life in general, it was called racking. Racking was basically shoplifting but the mentality was totally different.

Graffiti itself was a crime, it was not like today where it is part of popular culture and considered legitimate art. Back in the 1980s it was viewed as a scourge on society and blamed for shitty quality of life in many areas of New York city which couldn't be further from the truth. The truth is, Graffiti was the result of a shitty quality of life in New York City, not the other way around.

Oddly enough Graffiti today is accepted by mainstream culture and as I said in the introduction used by major corporate culture vultures like Nike, Adidas, Complex, Balenciaga, Louis Vuitton, the list goes on. And today, oddly enoough, illegal graffiti is probably a more serious crime than it was back then in terms of enforcement.

Back then you pretty much had to be caught doing it to be charged, today you just got to post something you painted illegally on social media. I guess some of today's enforcement elevation comes from technology but moreover a general interest in punishing the lower class that actually builds the culture while the upper class profits from it. In that frame of view not much has changed, I guess.

As I said, Graffiti was a crime, and was also time consuming, it was difficult to have a job and do graffiti, although people did sometimes but regardless if you had money or not, it didn't make sense to pay for spray paint and markers and clothes that would get destroyed or lost in order to commit a crime did it?

So back in the 1980s any real graffiti writer had to steal paint and supplies, had to trespass into train yards and tunnels, had to run from the law and be an outlaw at the same time (A sentiment voiced beautifully in the film Wild Style by Zoro, played by Lee), but it's true.

And graffiti was a gateway crime for many, for most. What started off as a desire to create art and/or see your name up in the streets where you lived and on the trains that you rode, grew into a compulsion to steal paint and supplies that became a compulsion to steal everything, because why not? Including cars and robbing other people and or businesses, homes, etc. Many people wound up doing long prison bids for living a life of crime that can be directly traced back to graffiti being their introduction to breaking the law.

To me, and many, you cannot consider yourself a true graffiti writer if you buy paint. At that point you cross over to being a street artist, and that distinction is an important one and a reason many graffiti writers lost interest as they got older because buying paint and doing legal graffiti just did not offer the same adrenaline-fueled rush and satisfaction. I am one of those people. Once I got tired of running from the law, I just lost interest in doing graffiti altogether for the most part. Sure, occasionally I still paint something, but for the most part it just isn't the same.

But that's not to say I don't still love and obsess about graffiti as part of who I am and what built me. True graffiti writers that let graffiti take over their lives will never truly get over it. Graffiti at one point for most true graffiti writers completely destroyed life, it led to court cases, fights and violence, friends becoming enemies, people damaging your parents' house, people always looking for you to hurt you, cops looking for you, etc. It was truly a lifestyle that was far from always enjoyable except for the rush of getting over. There was a rush when you got over racking, it filled you like a drug. There was a rush that filled your soul when you were painting graffiti in the middle of the night against all odds, there was a rush that filled you when you saw your name on a train or drove by it in the back of your parents car, and there was even a rush when writers knew who you were or wanted to kill you for going over them.

It is like a drug that rush, and graffiti was as much an addiction as it was a compulsion, and like many true addicts, you will never fully recover from that desire.

By early 1990 I was leaving for college, I gave away all of my remaining paint and supplies including a bunch of vintage cans and inks I had. My parents threw out the rest, all of my black books and a bunch of photos and army jackets etc. Something I never fully got over still today.

In 1991, while home for Christmas or Thanksgiving break I got caught up in an incident for which I was arrested and charged and was now looking at serious time in prison. It was a stupid thing that I am not going to go into in this book but it was something that so often happened to others and something that I will touch on in another story. One of the ways street kids from our generation wound up in prison was often getting caught up in bullshit that goes down on the block like fights and other things where you might not have been the one that was guilty of the most serious offenses, but the laws were structured in a way that they called it "Acting in concert" to the felony and you would catch the most serious charge anyway. After initially being stuck on Rikers Island waiting for my parents to raise my bail money, and my brother starting college as well, it was obvious I wouldn't be returning to my out of state school. I stayed in NYC for the remainder of 1992 to handle that case which ended rather amicably for me thanks to a good friend who helped out.

During the court case however, my attorney told me I needed to have a job for optics in case we go to trial. It was important that I didn't look like I was a slacker do nothing that was causing trouble. I got a job at a dry cleaner and met a local writer a few years younger than I was, named Sean. He was a fan of sorts of some of the older writers he grew up around, me being one of them. He wanted to start doing graffiti in a larger sense and I was just clearing up that court case.

During that court case I was beating myself up because I could have gotten caught racking and gotten caught writing 30 times each and still be in less trouble than I am now where I was facing 25 years and initial offers to settle that included 2 years of prison time upstate. I always said how badly I wished I could just turn back the clock and stick with graffiti. When the case was resolved and I did not have to do any jail time I was elated, I called my brother who was in Atlanta at the time for school and we immediately decided we were going to make a graffiti comeback in 1993.

That coupled with our new friend Sean was all of the motivation we needed.

But now was the hard part. After being removed from graffiti and the lifestyle for almost 2 years it was hard to get started because we had no paint.

My brother was home for Christmas in 1992 and we were out at Roosevelt Field mall with my now wife and her best friend Jhomy. Roosevelt Field Mall had a Woolworth in it at that time and we found ourselves in the basement of the store near the paint. My brother and I decided at that moment we were going to start this life again and started stuffing can after can into our winter jackets, getting about 6 each right when our friend Jhomy, who didn't know much about us yet turned the corner. She was appalled when she realized what we were doing to which my brother looks at her and says, "I know it's wrong Jhomy, but it must be done."

Today, she adds to this story that we grabbed her some hair care products on the way out to shut her up, and it worked. Bribery, not flattery, will get you everywhere.

But on this night, we realized, it was going to be on for the upcoming year and we needed to start racking.

When my brother returned to college, we drove down there a couple of weeks later and stayed with him, it was almost spring break and our girls were all going to be in

Daytona beach so we started racking in all of the stores around Atlanta and other parts of Georgia and then drove towards Daytona beach.

We developed a scheme where we would ask for "Jungle Green" Krylon, or "Icy Grape", both long discontinued colors as we were on our way out of the hardware stores each time with paint already on us, they would say they didn't have it off course and then we would ask them to point us towards the next nearest hardware store. And we did this shuffle all the way to Daytona beach, going from local hardware store to local hardware store over a two week span eventually amassing about 600 cans back in his college room. We would later bring these back up to NYC in a Van because they would not fit into the trunk of a car with our luggage.

When you are doing graffiti, it is always an advantage and a luxury to never have to go get paint. We linked up with the DBI crew that year and started smashing together and they were starting to rack more and more just because they saw how we always had paint ready to go.

We would take every opportunity to always acquire more. One day we were with some people in Fresh Meadows going to a movie, we ducked into a local store to kill time, by then paint in that area was always behind lock and key because of all of the graffiti writers stealing it, but on this particular night they were getting ready to load the locked cabinets with new inventory and they stacked case after case of "American Accents" paints in the aisle. Droma looked at me and said the Beastie Boys line "There was a case in the place and we went right through it" as he started ripping open the boxes, we put 12 cans each in the trunk of our car that night before going into the movies. And that's just the way life was for graffiti writers. Racking became such a necessary evil that it ceased to feel wrong.

Looking back now I realize what scumbags we were as I look at shoplifters today and pass judgment, but at the end of the day we are all just making our way in this world.

It wasn't just limited to paint, I mention in another story I was racking and selling jackets making a street living before I even had a car, and then once I got a car, you'd rack other things too that you could sell like batteries, film, etc. to generate gas money, food money and more. Some kids I grew up with even used to rack fresh sliced cold cuts and seafood. They would order the cold cuts or lobsters at the butcher counter and then stuff that into their bags or jackets and set up on the side of the road and sell lobsters. I am not joking that is 100% true. Funny as it sounds.

If you were on a long haul racking mission, we found out the hard way that you had better remove labels and peel off tags in between stops because if you were to get pulled over or arrested, the cops would see all of the stores you went to and then would get all of them to press charges making the case multiple complainants and increasing the value threshold to more serious charges.

Even then, after a while we'd get lazy again and stop doing that and just take the risks.

Chapter 5

ARMY JACKET

If you were a graffiti writer in the 1980s, there is a very good chance you wore a M-65 Field Army Jacket at one point or another. The common colors were dark green and black, sometimes they could have been navy but to my recollection all of the ones I owned were green or black, and one I think was like oiled or some kind of coated for water resistance although I only vaguely can recall that one.

In this jacket you could conceal cans in the sleeves very easily, both for racking purposes from a store, and for carrying cans in the middle of the night purposes. Sometimes the quickest way to get stopped and searched by a random cop was to be walking with a bookbag on in the middle of the night.

The jacket had a ton of pockets where you could put ink and markers, caps, weapons and mace. Yes, most graffiti writers carried weapons at one point in the 1980s. The jackets were stealthy, being 100% cotton canvas, they made no sound, they were also made by design to limit visibility, we spent much of our time lurking in the shadows under the cover of night. And these were real army jackets, from army surplus, not from the gap or urban outfitters, but real surplus left over from wars. And you wore an army jacket because you were a graff soldier in a game that had very little reward outside of recognition of some of your peers, there was no financial upside, no parlaying this into a career in graphics, sure some famous writers did make money back then, but I could count on my fingers how many. You did it for the love of the process and being an outlaw, it was a fuck you to your parents, society, and other writers.

If someone you didn't know asked you if you wrote graffiti, most of the time the response was no unless you were ready to throw down at that moment with an unknown adversary. The mere asking of that question was considered an act of aggression in most instances, and someone approaching you saying, "What you write?" was the equivalent of someone saying "What are you looking at?" today. It was a moment in time in this universe that will never be replicated.

The jackets were fairly warm even though they were not lined. I believe there was a lining available but no one I knew wore the lining. Instead, what we did was wear a nice thick zip hoodie underneath this army jacket, with just that hoodie and the field jacket, we could withstand the coldest of NYC nights in the dead of winter, I don't remember ever really being cold other than my hands.

And this would go on to become the uniform on New York City Street at the time and going forward, real street, well beyond graffiti. An online friend of mine reminded me that it became such universal street trooper wear that undercover police would start to wear the same thing, hoodie and all by the 1990's just so they would blend in with real street dudes doing real street things.

Another advantage of the army jacket was it did not attract attention, you were more likely to be mistaken for a homeless war vet if someone saw you standing in an alley at 2am that you were to be considered a target of stick-up kids or police searches. The same was not true if you were wearing a goose down jacket, or a leather bomber, or most other types of outerwear.

That, believe it or not, was a huge consideration when you were riding trains through one of the roughest cities in the world at the roughest times in history at all hours of the night alone or in very small groups.

In the mid-eighties I started racking goose down jackets, for those that might be reading but completely unfamiliar with the terminology of the time, racking meant shoplifting and is how real graffiti writers of the day got their supplies and clothing, it was part of the lifestyle.

I did not rack the goose down jackets to wear, although I did wear them from time to time if I went to a club or something like that. I racked them to sell and I was damn good at it. Two of the most popular were Macy's Club Room goose ski jackets and Triple Fat Goose ski jackets, I also used to have a place to get leather bombers. Many writers bought jackets from me, some I even gave away and some said they would pay me later and I never saw them again, which is what often happens when you extend people credit in life of any kind.

But as I said before, the stick-up kids would come looking to rob you if they saw you out in an expensive goose jacket, and two of the well-known writers I sold them to did in fact get robbed for them, at least one of the robberies happened in Chino BYI's building.

One story even goes, Chino and two other writers were

on the elevator up when two neighborhood kids got on with them. When Chino and friends got to their floor Chino stepped off and as the last one of his friends went to step off, they pulled him back into the elevator and the doors closed. By the time Chino and them ran down to the bottom to try to help this guy the stick-up kids were gone and this guy was standing there sneaker-less and jacketless. In both instances I gave them new jackets free of charge.

I even on rare occasions got "Troop" jackets which were leather jackets and highly controversial because of the amount of people that got killed in robberies for those jackets, it was considered an act of bravado to wear one out on the streets at one point. I rarely wore it for this reason. I couldn't rack these in the traditional way however because they were tough to get and heavily guarded. I would purchase them at The Coliseum in Jamaica using proceeds from other jackets and items I racked and sold.

Chapter 6

MOHAWKS AND PIZZA IN BROOKLYN; April 1987

In early 1987 I had just been given an old late 70's Honda by my dad as my first car, I was 17 years old at the
time and just got my license. My dad did not want to be
giving me a car, nor was he the type, but he didn't want
me ever asking to drive his Cadillac. He had a good
friend that was a bit of a mobbed-up car dealer, so the
guy gave him a car to give me. It was a decent car, being
a Honda, it was very reliable.

One evening me and my friend Angel, went down to
Brooklyn to meet some writers and we got there early.
With time to kill we went into a Clinton Hill pizzeria to
grab a couple of slices. Was it called Clinton Hill back
then? I honestly don't remember, it was an area between

Park Slope and Ft. Greene, which I think now is referred to as Clinton Hill.

My friend was known as Angel because that's what he wrote on walls, and trains and pretty much everything he came across. I was known as Stane for the same reasons. Everyone in these stories and pretty much in our lives at this point was known solely as a name other than their birthnames, it was very common in NYC. Even people that weren't graffiti writers at this time had nicknames like Little Johnnie, Bobbie Irish, Seal, Jason Maxima, etc.

My friend Angel and I both had mohawks, like the Sid Vicious - 8 inch tall shaved everywhere else mohawks, and they were lying flat this particular night but were visibly mohawks none the less. We were also in army jackets and dark jeans, with combat boots on and had writing of band names and tags on some of our clothes. This would not have been such a strange sight if were in the village in the mid to later 1980s, but in certain parts of Brooklyn and Queens, it made us stand out, a little too much sometimes.

On this particular day we parked and got out, it was about 7pm. We walked into this place and in the first two booths were about six older guys, probably about mid-twenties in age and a mixed bag of characters and ethnicities, all of which had a bit of the New York City hard-rock look to them. Some gold fronts, some shaved parts in their hair, some jewelry, but mostly loud. They noticeably got quieter when we walked in. The feeling that they were staring at us was palpable, but still we ordered our food, to go of course, and waited for it.

"What the fuck are you guys supposed to be?" quipped one of the guys from the booth near the door. All of them facing us now.

"Nothing" said Angel "Just rocking out, ya know?"

The group laughed and started muttering to themselves as the guy behind the counter put our two cups of coke and two white bags with the paper plate and the slices on the counter.

Oddly enough this little detail was just so New York, and "Old" New York, they would put the slices on a white paper plate and slide them into a white bag, then fold the end of the bag in towards the top of the pizza and you would carry the slices out sideways. Now, most places will give you to go slices in a box, although in NYC you will still get the bag from real pizzerias.

We grab our food and make the awkward walk back past this group who are now laughing at us aloud.

As my hand reached the door handle to push it open, "You guys faggots?" says that same guy. Because picking on two 17 year olds was just so typical in NYC at this time.

I push the door open as Angel throws his soda on them "Fuck you!" he screams. And like in a movie, the chase was on! We couldn't get out the door fast enough, and they couldn't get out of those booths fast enough. We ran down the entire block with all of them about 40 yards behind us, we got to my car and in almost cliché fashion Angel was yelling "Open the door, open the fucking door!"

We got the doors open as I backed to clear the car in front of me to pull out when they all ran up to the car pounding on the windows, two of them standing in front of the car with their hands on the hood as if they could hold the car in place, they were now trying to break the windows with their fists.

"Run them over!" screams Angel at the top of his lungs in the chaos, everything slowed down in my head as I looked at this vicious mob trying to get in my car before thinking to myself, what choice do I have here? I put the car in drive and floored it sending the two standing in front of it up over the hood and tumbling over the top and rolling off the back, we sped off with about three of them chasing us in the street.

Holy shit we exclaimed to each other, "what the fuck just happened?!" I exclaimed, "Just keep driving …" replied Angel. So we did.

Oddly enough we kept the pizza, but not the drinks, we ate the slices and about half an hour later met up with three older writers. Chino, our good friend, and two older writers not nearly as friendly, but we were cool with them. We will call these two WRITER X and WRITER Y for this story.

We pulled up to the corner and there they were waiting for us. We jumped out of the car yelling like kids on a Christmas morning so excited to tell the tale of what just transpired.

The three of them were like "Yo! What the fuck, lets go fuck those dudes up!" That was quite literally what Writer X and Writer Y said, Chino was down with it, but he wasn't as overly excited about the situation. "Yeah?" Angel said. Chino was 2 years older than us, Writer X and Writer Y were both even older than Chino, about 24 at the time and both somewhat known for their propensity to get involved in fights, and all three were large; much bigger than the average person, so what could go wrong?

I'll tell you what can go wrong, and what did go wrong.

We pulled back into that neighborhood and found the six of those guys with another three or four newcomers standing on a corner telling their version of the events of that evening, they were also excited and looking for a fight when what happens? The exact guys they were talking about pull back up and Writer X and Writer Y immediately jump out with Chino, they go over to them.

It turns out Chino knows a couple of them and they start talking and those guys tell them that their beef is not with them but instead their beef is with us.

And they tell them to set up one on one fights with the two older guys that we put over the car. These two were now standing right outside our car punching our windows again while the three of the older writers we pulled up with were talking to the group.

Chino comes over and tells us what is going on.

"Fight this guy one on one?" I said. "No fucking way." I

said.

Look, I already hit the dude with my car, as far as I am concerned, I won, and besides, I was not a person particularly interested in fights. I would fight when I had to defend myself, I never in my life have been slapped or mushed by another man and stood there without swinging, I never have been robbed where I didn't go down swinging. But to just arbitrarily fight a one on one with a man I just hit with my car when it was these guys that wanted to come back to "Fuck them up" themselves? Nah, not my thing, I refused. And Angel at first said he wasn't interested as well. Then Writer X comes over to the car, "Guys, get the fuck out here and fight these guys."

"Nope. Why would I, you wanted to come back here, you fight them" I responded. "You are making me look like a punk because you're my boy and you are acting like a little bitch." He said.

"I'll fight him, I ain't no punk" said Angel, and Angel got out to fight. Chino leaned into the car window, he did not look thrilled with the turn of events.

I started the car, Chino opened the passenger door. I Stood up and took a picture as the fight started, the fight quickly got out of control as the dude was much bigger and older than Angel, Angel pulled out what we used to call a "Hole Puncher" it was a mini self-defense baton that had two spikes that would fit between your knuckles, and you would literally punch holes in people.

The situation deteriorated quickly, others started swinging on Angel, it was no longer a one on one. He moved toward my car as I started to pull out. Chino got in, we pulled up to Angel who was moving away from the crowd swinging on him, with the door open Angel fell into Chino's lap and Chino Held him as we sped off, door still open and Angels legs hanging out of the car. We got to the end of the block, just enough distance away from the pursuing crowd, Angel got in the back seat, we left. We left Writer X and Writer Y there.

We went into the village and got ourselves back together. I took another photo from that night. In this pic is Angel and Chino at a then Broadway staple, Chino Latino. We couldn't afford to eat there though; we just ate snacks and beers from the corner store.

There was some significant aftermath of this night in my relationship with Writer X, my relationship with Writer Y was not affected. Chino till this day remains one of my closest friends, separated by thousands of miles for the past couple decades we still catch up every time I am in New York City and we stay in touch online. Angel is still one of my oldest friends. I gave the picture of the actual fight to Angel, my parents threw away that negative with a bunch of other stuff a few years later.

To see these photos and others go to my Instagram stories and posts - @bronxscienceog

Chapter 7

PROXIMITY, OR LACK THERE OF

There were several notable writers to come out of Bayside queens, Duel and Angel probably being the most
well-known, others, including myself to a lesser extent.
Partially due to the types of things we wrote on, Duel
killed streets and highways in our vicinity in the late
1980s into the 1990's and so did Angel, Angel also had a
lot of trains, I mostly hit trains in the 1980s and did a lot
of pieces and some highways in the early 1990s when I
wasn't in court.

Hitting streets and Highways hard had its advantages,
younger writers that did not ride subways at the time
saw your work from the back of their parent's cars, they

remember you as a teenager having never ridden on subways. I started hitting subways in 1985 and hit mostly that until 1988 so anything I hit during those years was gone by 1988, with no remnants or work visible to a much wider audience that would see the streets and highways into the 1990s.

In simpler terms, the only people that will remember you up on subways were other train riding graffiti writers, as opposed to almost everyone growing up in a neighborhood remembers a throw-up on a particular corner or intersection whether they wrote or not.

But for writers, the goal was always subways, all writers wanted to hit subways and in Bayside that wasn't the easiest thing to do. The nearest subway stopped almost 3 miles West of Bayside, and another about 3 miles South. Those trains that stopped and were parked closest to Bayside, the E/F and the 7 were also amongst the first lines to stop running with any graffiti on them and were largely clean by 1985/6 making it even more of a journey to get to the nearest trains to participate. For Bayside writers the next nearest locations were in Ridgewood at the M Yard which had its own neighborhood kids hanging out, or the RRs in Astoria, two places most kids from Bayside had rarely ever been.

For most Bayside graffiti writers, with a few exceptions, getting up on trains was not a reality or an option they even had. Angel got down with QV RIS early on in 1984 and started hitting trains with them and hanging out in Woodside and areas where trains were more readily available. For me it was attending Bronx Science that opened that door. I started Bronx Science in 1983 and up until that point had never really ridden on graffitied trains, well maybe once or twice with my dad or uncle going to a ballgame or into my dad's job in Manhattan.

But actually riding the train everyday into school through Queens, into Manhattan and up into the Bronx changed everything. It was tangible, it was already something I wanted to do after seeing the book "Subway Art" but something I still had no clue about.

Oddly enough, the Bronx was literally three or four miles away from my house across the bay over the Throgs Neck Bridge, but by train it was a 90 minute ride through three boroughs to get there. There were no trains that connect Queens to the Bronx without Manhattan as a go between.

On top of that Bronx Science was directly across 205th street from the D Train yard, a yard I only went in twice. Once during a school day and did not write on anything after someone showed me how to squeeze through from the back of the elevated 4 platform on Jerome Ave. and one time I wound up there early at night after school and did do a throw up in the back corner on one of the trains that always seemed to be there.

The thought of making that trek all the way up there once I got home to go bombing was just unthinkable when I was 14 or 15. The Bronx looked pretty scary back then in 1984, the entire ride up Jerome Ave on the 4 train was burnt out abandoned buildings, most of which were smashed with Graffiti by 1985, Cope, Trim, Quik KD, LIL MAN and others.

At school, three of my good friends were Ray and Alex, and Mike. They wrote Jere, Dos, and Zerk respectively. Mike lived in Flushing and we hung out with him outside of school with his boys Dave and Hardy and skated near the McDonalds on Northern Blvd. Jere and Dos lived in Jackson Heights and Elmhurst and we started getting more into graffiti in 1985, our initial friendship started with punk rock and hardcore music. Jere started DMS, the Doc Marten Squad in 1986 and the three of us were good friends often hanging out in Jackson Heights with the 7 line writer Myse and others.

One day in 1985 Jere said to me he knew where they parked RR trains in Astoria and later that night, he took me and Nim there. It was the center elevated track from the first or second station after Queensborough Plaza towards Astoria and it ran through every station almost into Ditmars. The Station we went in was 36th, they had these elevated metal runners or track separators that separated the center track from the two active lanes, and if you stood on these in the station, you could reach the whole train from top to bottom. Seemed like a good thing to stand on and paint up high, later I found out from other writers that it was extremely frowned upon in the graff community to hit the lay-up in the station like that because you could be spotted and burn out the lay-up. But at the time we knew no better and Nim and I just went there a couple times a week and did a couple throw ups each.

When I first met Angel later that year he said how shocked he was when he saw Nim and myself, two local Bayside kids, running on the RRs with floaters and laughed when he found out we were hitting Astoria in the station.

For people not familiar with the subway system and how it works, the center track was an express track, during rush hours trains would switch onto this track to skip stations, but at night these center tracks on many train lines were packed end to end with trains parked overnight through station after station. Part of the logic being at the start of the next rush hour the additional trains were already scrambled out to all areas as opposed to having to send them out from the main yard locations which would make the wait for the additional trains further down the lines too long for passengers.

Eventually we started walking out onto the elevated tracks between the stations, it was very scary at first, very windy, the apartments that lined the tracks had dark windows in the middle of the night and faced directly at you, the trains in the center rattled in the wind, you had to watch for upcoming trains in the distance and squeeze in between cars to hide when it passed so they didn't call the cops. All while 50 feet above the street below walking on rotting 1" thick planks of flexible wood that spanned 6 feet between steel beams. If you dropped a can or accidentally kicked the one you put down while switching colors it would sometimes fall through the tracks making a loud noise as it crashed into parked cars on the street below.

And on top of all of this sometimes you would see other people coming down the tracks, sometimes writers or cops but back then I often didn't wait to find out because writers were not friendly for the most part and obviously if it was cops or workers you aren't supposed to be there, so now you are running down this weathered wood plank platform watching for oncoming trains, stranded between stations and sometimes you had to know how to climb down into the structure below, and use the rivets to ladder your way down to the street below. Something a writer Form/Kaser first showed me there. Those of you that write will know of Form, he kind of kinged those lines at the time with Ek Rank, PK, and others.

We once saw, I think it was ZOR BBK jump from the structure below the tracks there landing on top of the roof of a parked car crushing the roof when cops came in and we were all getting out of there in a hurry. It was crazy and dangerous.

What we did have near us in Bayside though was high-ways and street bombing. In very early 1986 Angel and I were walking from near Cardoza all the way up Springfield Blvd. to Union Turnpike, all the way down Union to Francis Lewis Blvd and all the way down past St. Francis Prep at the intersection of the Clearview Expressway and the Long Island Expressway. We had drippy pilot mops (Markers) and took tags on every light pole and mailbox along the way. Unknown to us, an off-duty police officer was following us for at least the last mile, watching us take at least 30 tags each and calling the on-duty police and setting up an ambush at the Long Island Expressway overpass.

When we crossed the bridge we were on opposite sides of the street bombing the poles as we walked, Angel was about ¾ of the way across, I was in the center. Four cop cars with their lights off and this off duty car all sped onto the bridge to close us off, Angel was close enough to the end that he went over the rail to the 10 foot drop to the side of the freeway below and took off, I was over the highest part of the roadway, jumping would have been fatal. Keep in mind this was when highway overpasses only had 3-foot-high rails, not those 8 foot curved chain links they have now.

The off-duty cop runs up to me and violently tackles me to the floor, picking me up and slamming me onto the hood of one of the police cars. Angel and I used to wear thick bicycle lock chains around our waists as belts, because of punk rock and because you could take it off and knock someone out with it.

When this cop slammed me onto the police hood the chain came out and scratched up the hood, he slams my head into the hood holding the chain splitting my face, a scar I still have on my lip today.

"What the fuck is this?!" he exclaims as he is breathing heavy and spitting into my face, he picks me up and throws me back down. It was a violent enough scene at about midnight that a passerby stopped his car at the corner and he ran down the overpass screaming "Hey! That's enough, he's a child goddamnit!" because I was 15 and small and looked young. The cop quickly shoves his badge in the guy's face and tells him to mind his business, the guy looks at me and without speaking mouths the words "Are you ok?"

It was a touching bit of humanity at a time when I experienced very little, it still chokes me up today, good people around in that fucking crazy city back then?

I was scared but didn't really see the situation getting any better if I dragged this guy into it so I nodded to insinuate "Yes" as I was being held down by the cops on the hood and he turned and walked back to his car.

"Who's your friend?" they said.

"Some homeless guy that lives by Alley Pond." I Said.

"Whats his name?"

"Steven" I said.

They pulled out a bunch of Angel and Stane stickers we wrote out together from one of the army jacket pockets, "Is that Angel?"

"I dunno" I screamed, "Just leave me the fuck alone!"

They took me back to the 111th station and asked if I was in high school as they processed me and were getting ready to call my mom, I was 15 there should have been no arrest, but they said they were under pressure to prosecute juveniles in court for graffiti at the time. I told him I went to Bronx Science.

"Bullshit!" he said.

They were pissed and this off duty cop tried to tally up damage from all of the tags we took that night and for the ones on the mailboxes he brought in some federal paperwork. My mom came to get me and I had one court date, they gave me 10 hours of community service which I did at flushing meadow park, they also stipulated that I needed to participate in an after school program or get a job of some sort, which my dad got me with a friend of his in Manhattan packaging natural pet food. The brand was still around until not that long ago – Doctor Harvey's.

While doing community service that spring, they used to load us on a bus and bring us out to different parts of the park near the world's fair grounds and pick up trash or paint a weathered fence. Because I was 15 years old, I was limited to 2-hour days so I had to go 5 times.

The second day the bus driver who was one of the parks employees that ran the Flushing Community Service program asks me what I did. "Graffiti" I said.

"Ahhh, I remember I had a guy in here last year 'The Ghost', he stopped coming after the second day, do you know the Ghost?"

"Not yet" I said, "but we have friends in common". I would meet Ghost later that year.

But before I met him one day I asked Cro why Wes was in RIS and I wasn't, it was supposedly a closed crew by 1986 and they weren't going to let anyone else down, I bombed with Gato, Neo, Cro, Wes, Angel, was friends with old school Dasher RIS, and I fought alongside them. I was down in other major crews at this point. Cro told me Wes goes and bombs the Es and Fs by himself, maybe your just not dedicated enough yet. He probably told me this to shut me up but, I took it as a challenge.

That night I went to Astoria lay-ups at midnight, it was cold and windy, I took the lonely walk along the rattling train, trains also make noises like they are turning on and off and loud compressors blast with a hiss sometimes. The dark ominous apartment windows were-watching, it gets in your head sometimes when you are alone.

I took out two Rusto almonds and started doing fill in after fill in down the train about midway between stations, probably about five or six of them. It was very windy and much of the paint was missing the train which was an RR flat. Those trains were perfect to write on, almost black and rust colored by the buff acid, the white fill ins almost glowed in contrast. I outlined them with Rusto burgandy then walked back to the station, crossed the tracks and climbed back onto the platform.

I waited right there for the next train to come take me home. I looked down the layup with a sense of pride at my graffiti, the only legible graffiti on the buffed train at the moment.

It would be another year before I would start bombing 57th by myself, but for the time being at least, no one could ever say that again to me, I did go bombing by myself.

Another fall out from that arrest on the overpass for the marker tags, as I mentioned, was the job sponsor at the pet food company for the court case. I think this was a result of the federal charge for the mailboxes.

I would take the train into Manhattan every mid-day

and start work at 1 to 6, I think that might have been the max hours I could work at 15 or 16.

Cro wanted to start doing insides on the ridgie trains that were replacing the RRs as the lines were crossing over to the B's around that time.

After morning rush hour, they would park trains on the center tracks again all the way out to Ditmars, and from 10am-2pm it was open season on those ridgies. Sure there were people on the platforms and in the neighboring windows but once you snuck onto the locked train (Yes we had keys) you could walk inside and between cars the whole way from station to station taking tags and destroying the insides.

First thing I would do when I got inside the train was sit down, take out a bottle of ink, open the marker and fill it until it was overflowing and a dripping mess. Then it was on, rip off posters, write on everything in every spot available; go over faded tags, car after car after car for two hours before going into work covered in ink.

After about the third day we ran into Zor and Nash BBK who had a gun. My first thought was fuck lets run! But it turns out it was a BB Gun and they would shoot out windows and just be stupid with it so we all got along. Then we started meeting up there every day to write on the insides, and they used to like to make jokes and do things like open the passenger doors on the train out in the middle of the lay-up scaring the shit out of us and exposing us to the neighboring apartment or office windows that were occupied now as it was broad daylight. It was a lot of fun.

Eventually after you get over on a spot enough, commuters start to complain about wet ink on the trains. Or the conductors get tired of getting on the train to pull out and finding posters ripped down and doors left open and tags still wet, etc.

This is when a lay-up gets burnt out or "Hot" as they called it. It wasn't long before one morning Cro and I did our usual, we crossed the tracks right after the train left taking the passengers from the platform with it. We climbed up in between cars, and got inside the train, I sat down and Cro sat across from me, I took out my ink and was filling my marker, we heard the train door opening at the other end of the train, but assumed it was Zor and Nash. By the time we looked up two police officers with badges on their necks and a worker were in the fucking car with us!

Cro immediately jumped back out between cars, I threw the ink towards them and followed Cro, the first cop tried to grab me as he chased but he got hung up on the accordian brace in between cars that prevents people from doing exactly this. He falls onto the tracks as Cro runs down the stairs and out of the station, I was several steps behind Cro and still on the tracks with two cops in close pursuit, I jumped onto the platform, so did the cops, the platform was starting to fill up again with passengers for the next train, they looked on as I ran as fast as humanly possible past them with the cops right behind me. I came to the railing to the stairs and didn't think I had enough time to reach the end and turn so I leapt over the high side of the rail landing about 14 feet below on the steps, one of my ankles half hits a step and shatters, I run/hop out the station and slide immediately under an auto service riot gate that is partially open, the guy inside the auto shop sees me, a filthy hurt kid, he hears the cops he knows what's up.

"Bathroom?" I say with a wince.

He points towards a door while watching the feet run around outside past the slightly open gate I slid under. "Right there" he says.

I come out a few minutes later hopping in excruciating pain and ask to use the phone and he lets me. I call my dad and ask him to take me to the hospital, he calls Harvey and tells him I won't be at work this week.

My ankle was fractured in two places, I still walk with a limp today, I was in a cast for almost 3 months, and this is the price we paid for graffiti.

Chapter 8

THE LONGEST WALK

What is the longest walk you've ever gone on? And what was the reason?

In the mid 1980s at 15 and 16 years of age we often found ourselves far from home with no means of transportation, and if you wanted to go someplace a train didn't go, often that meant walking it. You couldn't get on a bus without a school pass or fare for the most part, neither of which we had often at night.

I mean we always kept that emergency token or fare on us but that was end of night stuff to get home, we couldn't use that money to travel while we were out because eventually, we'd be stranded.

But even with an emergency fare on me, I used to regularly walk home from Main Street Flushing at the end of the 7 line where the Q13 stops for Bayside. The bus stopped running late each night, and I had no alternative if the bus wasn't running.

My mom was often pissed at me for not coming home the previous night or something and wouldn't answer the phone.

That was a pretty long walk, probably like 2 miles, took like 45 minutes or so, and it sucked, especially after a long night of hanging out, partying, bombing, etc. Sometimes she would answer the phone though, and then she'd be super pissed when she pulled up at 4am to get her delinquent son from a street corner. But at least I didn't have to walk on those nights!

Another reason to walk would be to go bombing with markers or spray paint, sometimes you would just head out on foot writing on everything in your path and just walk until you ran out of paint or ink.

One such night in 1986, it was Cro RIS, Wes RIS and myself and we were coming from Wes' house about 9pm and had a few cans each. We walked down Northern Blvd toward Shea Stadium and hopped down onto the highway and just walked and did throw ups and tags the whole way, we walked all the way from Levitt's Field past La Guardia Airport through Elmhurst eventually winding up underneath the 7 line in Jackson Heights near USA Skates.

That was a long walk, probably like 4 miles, or more, not entirely sure of our route anymore. We walked right on the highway, past those gas stations on the highway by the world's fair marina and La Guardia that sat closed and vacant most of my life until the 2000's, we wrote on those, we wrote on every wall and pillar, we wrote on everything along the way.

It was Saturday night and by the time we got near USA Skates it was about 2am, the time it was letting out, we hopped the turnstile up onto the elevated 7 line platform and were waiting for the train when we could see the Skate club was letting out below; immediately realizing it was a bad idea being here, but it was too late. Cro was sitting on the edge of the platform with his legs dangling onto the tracks.

It was known by us at that time that the crowd from that club contained all sorts of want to be hard rocks and local graffiti writers that we were already going over, and we knew better. I don't think any of us even had a watch back then and we had no idea our timing would be so bad as we approached. Besides what choice did we have at this point? There was no one to call.

That's the thing about this decade, you were on your own, truly.

Cro was sitting on the platform, legs dangling, I was standing about five yards down from him and Wes was leaning against the corrugated metal wall. The platform was completely empty except for us and in the early spring it is chilly late at night, and you could feel the wind blowing on your hair and face. Looking down the tracks in either direction was also very quiet, you could see red signal lights at the utility boxes and the next stations off in the distance, but it was motionless. There was always something a bit magical looking down the perspective of the tracks going off into the distance at night. Still today, even looking down the perspective of the tracks disappearing into a train tunnel, it is mysterious and inviting, at least to me it is.

The night sky looked nice from up there too, especially if you looked West towards Manhattan, the skyline lit and making you feel part of the city you lived in, we were truly parts of this city, not isolated in cars and locked away in our homes but the city was living and breathing in us. Sounds a little mushy now but it was a sense of contentment that I don't know much in my adult life. There was no longing for anything I didn't have other than more cans so I could spend more time out at night writing on the city we loved.

The silence would start to break when we could hear crowds letting out from the popular skating rink and nightclub below, we stood there watching the dozens of kids run up the stairs onto the platform we had just previously felt like was our own. It's a weird feeling of vulnerability when a place you are occupying is now being infiltrated by potential adversaries, unless you have been in that situation it is very hard to describe the feeling when you get "run up on."

Things slow down, you start to have a realization of specific details, your heartbeat speeds up to a pounding as your adrenaline puts you into a fight or flight mode, flight is usually not an option when your boys are there or in danger, so that thought doesn't really cross your mind. It's going to be a fight, in most cases.

Fear is there, and usually you look toward the person in your group who has been in this situation the most, you follow their cues. In this case Cro was a year or two older than us and one of the early RIS crew, he had been in many fights before, more than us.

The kids from the club were dressed in b-boy attire and dress clothes popular at the time, the three of us were in army jackets, needless to say we didn't blend in.

Still no trains in sight, nothing was coming to break the tension of this moment.

I look toward Cro to see what he is going to do; he is

still sitting with his feet dangling off above the tracks as two kids walk right up behind him, getting real close. They are looking down at him with their knees in a position near him that they could easily nudge him down onto the tracks. Things move slowly compared to the racing of your heartbeat, that feeling just before you know shit is about to pop off.

Cro turns his head to look up at them acknowledging that they are there, and he quickly jumps to his feet. He's now nose to nose with the kid whose friends gather around in a circle with me just on the outside of it. The kid smiles at Cro and starts going through Cro's pockets on his army jacket to rob him. Cro reaches into his right pocket and grabs a padlock that he took off one of the gates in the transit system with his keys, he carried it as a weapon. He pulls it out and quickly punches the one kid sending him falling backward. Cro was so close to the edge of the platform when he threw that punch there was no place for him to back up to even assume a full fighting stance, he steps off the platform and lands on his feet on the tracks.

The kid closest to me now turns to grab me as I shove him into the crowd and I follow Cro onto the tracks. But remember Wes? He was back against the wall and now the crowd is between Cro and I and him, he fights his way through the crowd to get to us, they aren't going to let him onto the tracks, they start swinging on him, his glasses fall off as they wrestle him to the floor, Cro and I now each have one of his legs.

We yank Wes onto the tracks and the three of us start running down the elevated tracks towards the Woodside station, two of these kids start to give chase but aren't immediately comfortable on the tracks and just stand there. They look back and see the train is approaching so they get back onto the platform with the others to take the train to beat us to the next station. We make it about a third of the way out on this elevated train track and stop behind the first utility box. The train passes us with all of these kids on the train looking out the brightly lit windows at us trying to get to the next station where they will be waiting. We flip them off hiding behind the utility box so the conductor doesn't stop the train if he sees us.

We run back towards the platform we just left, looking back we can see them at the Woodside Station, a couple of them now on the tracks realizing we are getting away.

Our lead is huge, we run through the station on the elevated track to the next station, and then exit to the street and take the remaining walk on the Roosevelt Ave Bridge above the 7 train yard and the Van Wyck past Shea Stadium on Roosevelt to Main Street.

That night is what felt like the longest walk to me. There were several others close, but I think overall this was it.

At Main Street we said goodnight to each other, Cro turned right down towards Kissena Blvd, Wes turned left back toward Northern Blvd. And I walk straight up Roosevelt towards Bayside going into an all-night store with my last dollars to get change to call my mom to see if she would come get me because the bus was no longer running at this hour. I also bought a drink in a glass bottle because I hadn't had anything to drink in five hours and have been sweating and running for my life the entire night. I often bought a glass bottle of beer or soda at this station because the bottle itself made a great weapon. My nights often ended right here alone and at this hour and it was deserted.

I walked across the silent street to the pay phone and picked up the receiver to make the call, but before I could dial I hear in a stern voice behind me "Yo, what you write?"

Oh my fucking god I thought to myself because I was running on empty at this point, and alone. I turned around and there was a white dude that kind of looked like a cop standing there.

"What? No, I don't write." I said.

"Yes you do, I saw you, what do you write?"

"Saw me where?" I said.

"Doing throw ups on the highway with Cro and Wes."

Now I'm completely confused and scared, I mean where the fuck did this guy come from? How did he see us and how does he know who Cro and Wes were?

He's sensing my anguish now and decides to let me off the hook.

"I was driving by with Seen, PJay and Cap and we saw you guys, we tried to turn around, but you were all gone." He said.

108

Like something out of the much later to come movie
The Matrix, he holds out his hand for a handshake -

"Whats up Stane" he says. "Cro told me a lot about you,
I'm Neo."

And that is how I met NEO NOG RIS.

At the time Neo was a legend, he was original RIS and
QV and his crew NOG was envied by almost all flushing
and Bayside writers, only a select few got down early on.
He was close with Cap MPC and other legendary Bronx
Writers, he had been doing pieces and throw ups on
trains going back as far as 1979.

Meeting Neo at this time was huge and something I had
been looking forward to.

I wound up not calling my mom and hung out with Neo
for another hour or so, just talking as the sun came up.
The Q13 was running by now and I took the bus back to
Bayside.

Chapter 9

57th STREET

Neighborhoods mattered when it came to navigating
the city by train and bus at this time. As I've mentioned
before, coming from Bayside and Flushing we didn't
have a home lay-up by 1985ish as the 7 line and the Es
and Fs were amongst the first trains to run mostly clean,
they were still being hit in 1985 sure, but by 1986 they
ran almost no graffiti on those lines.

Chino used to call certain neighborhoods "Russian"
neighborhoods back then and the first couple of times I
was wondering "How does he know?" I don't see many
Russian people here but what he meant was "Rushin"

as in you will get rushed if the locals catch you walking thru there, and he was right.

In most cases, most larger train yards and lay-ups had their own local writers and neighborhood hard rocks that would guard them closely, certainly by 1985-1986, so the choices of where we could bomb had an element of danger sometimes in the selections. 175th was one of those, the Parkside Brooklyn Shuttle, New Lots, and many others. These weren't great options to hit and even if we did, it would be a get in and get out and don't go back for a bit kind of thing.

57th Street Layup was a well-guarded secret for many years. Neo, Gato, Cro and some RIS crew went there on occasion in 1986, and 357 crew went there, that was pretty much it and they did not go often yet. It only held two trains parked in the tunnels that connected the original N and R Tunnels to the newer JFK Train tunnels that ran under Central Park before heading towards Queens. Both of those parked trains however had platform height catwalks on one side making it a great place to do top to bottoms and floaters.

One reason it went relatively unhit and stayed so clean until 1986 was most other writers in Manhattan had other larger layups closer to them. The other was the neighborhood. These trains parked almost literally underneath the Plaza Hotel and Central Park by the zoo, right on 5th Ave. and the most protected and expensive real estate in New York City. There were cops around that area always and it wasn't really a great place for neighborhood kids to hang out. Also, the neighborhood kids there were rich and had better things to do besides hang out on the corner or in a layup.

Anyone remember the commercial jingle "Take the train to the plane?" from the mid-eighties? That was the MTA's new JFK Ding Dong which ran clean and they were intent to keep it that way. 57th Street did connect to the new tunnels and on occasion had JFK trains parked in there separate from the B and RR Trains in the 57th street part of the lay-up. Those trains were not to be hit for the most part and legend has it once Neo, Cro, and Gato and I think Scam got raided there and NEO ran through a train tunnel all the way to Queens, at least I think that was where that happened.

The tunnels were clean there, the lights were on, it connected to storage and workspace with staircases all underground beneath Central Park. You could enter through the storm/vent grates in the park behind the wall near 61st street which was adjacent to a rarely used sidewalk hatch. You could walk over from the 5th Ave station on the N line, which was a bit of a long walk from the lower tunnel before it connected upward right before the 57th Street station. It was easy to make if you entered the tunnel right after the train left the station.

There was another hatch on central park south in the park in the middle of a field right near the statue about midway between west and east side. This layup was in the shadow of the Ritz Carlton, the Trump Tower, The Pierre and the Sherry Netherland. When they first brought me there in late 1986, essentially, I never left and called it home. I would go there for the next year and a half many times per week or month. Many times, alone because it was so widely unknown any writers I

112

did run into knew me or knew someone that knew me, so there was rarely any fights or problems there. That's not to say new writers wouldn't come in there and get robbed, yes that did happen, I know it happened and who it happened to.

Writers from Brooklyn would call me up and ask me where I was smashing those top to bottoms on the B line, that's actually how I met Slick 501, I think Reuben was his name. He was a nice kid. Not many people knew about that place until later 1987 into 1988 when it got crowded. The B train largely parked in Brooklyn at the time and those lay-ups were a little bit hot. Part of graffiti always involved trying to figure out who hit what where.

By 1988 on any given night or day I would run into JA, Smith, Sane, Tekay, Chama, Fec, Kase 2, Seen TC5, Wane, Wips, Psycho FC, Joey TDS, and many others in there. Safe to say the secret was out, or maybe most of them knew about it but always had better layups to hit. The fact that this layup remained a bit of a hidden spot for so long made it one of the last to get shut down by the city.

1987 was the last great letter lines train year in my opinion, the RR flats still ran at the beginning and trains were still being buffed meaning that when you hit them your throw-ups or pieces glowed against the dark back drop with no other writers really up. The number lines probably had their last great year in 1986. By mid 1988 trains stopped being buffed and the graffiti just piled up and trains in general looked like trash, over bombed, too much graffiti over graffiti. By the end of that year, it got so crowded that people started going to lay-ups en-masse in these huge groups and if you went to 57th or 121st on the J line and did just a couple throw ups or a single piece these groups of writers would come in after you and cover the whole train and you'd be lucky to even see a corner of your piece sticking out from underneath. After seeing my throw ups like this a few times I called it quits on trains in mid 1988.

In 1987 express lane layups on the R line still laid up in Manhattan in the winter, the Astoria Layups still laid up and were hittable, there were options close to us, but those options became fewer and fewer in a very short time.

I think Seen declared "Graffiti Died" in 1982, can you imagine that? Old School train writers thought graffiti was dead 3 years before I even started writing on trains. Each generation of writers has their own perspective. I only hit one clean train on the Es and Fs in 1989 and one 7 train express track layup in 1990 and never got into the clean train movement. It was a valiant effort to keep subway graffiti alive, but it just wasn't the same for me and I lost interest.

Also, now being done with Bronx Science and having a car meant I did not ride trains as often, part of the allure of train graffiti to begin with is that feeling when you are waiting for your train, and it pulls in and BAM! You have your name all over it, it's hard to describe that feeling if you haven't felt it, but that was 90% of the juice.

In late 1988 I focused my energy into highways and a little bit of streets, then got into other crimes and hanging out with my friends and going to clubs more and more.

I would stop doing graffiti altogether in 1991 after getting arrested and having a potentially serious court case that took almost a year to clear up. I started racking again in 1993 and made a comeback in that year through 1994 with the DBI crew.

Chapter 10

IT WAS A SET UP, IT REALLY WAS

Writers often got set up at the hands of other writers, sometimes deliberately, sometimes other writers didn't really know what people intended when someone asked them to bring you to a lay-up to paint.

One of the most common questions I get from graffiti writers with knowledge of the era is why I was no longer part of the RIS crew since I was the first, and until later in 1988, one of only two put down in the mid-eighties after the initial forming of the crew and the early years. The crew was technically "Closed" at the time I got down and the intent was never to have any new members.

The timeline of graffiti is weird and with the expanse of the years it's hard to understand the perspective. When I met Ghost in 1986, he did not like me because I was a "Nu-jack." It was common perception at the time that anyone that started after 1983 was new and not part of the graffiti movement, but at the time Graffiti in its modern form had only existed for about 10 years total. And still, arriving in 1985 got you branded as new. When Ghost closed the crew by 1985, they were never going to let anyone else in after that.

It's a complicated issue why I was only in the crew for about 1 year, part of the story stems with the fight that is described in the "Mohawks and Pizza" story in this book, and certain people's perception that I fronted on a fight with a guy I already hit with my car.

The stakes are pretty high after you hit a guy with your car, even if you hit him only in self defense. That guy likely no longer wants to fight you but wants to kill you.

It wasn't a fight I felt like having and the truth is I never let anyone put their hands on me or rob me without swinging. That also being said I was not a fighter by any means, just a kid that had the smarts to survive in a city that was much tougher and somewhat older. The guy they wanted me to fight was 23 years old and bigger than me, I already put him over the hood of my car, what else did I have to prove?

When the shit hit the fan that night, I did not abandon my boy Angel who was fighting one of them, Chino and I strategically extracted him like Navy Seals on a mission and got him and us out of there to safety from a very angry mob.

Me not accepting that one on one fight that night is one version of the RIS story and why I got docked, another version goes like this. I was heavily bombing with RIS at the time, Cro, Gato, Ghost, Angel, Wes, Miro, and Neo, pretty much the core of the original members sans only a few. I got my license when I turned 17 and my dad got me an old beat-up Honda. My ego also got too large and I thought I was cool, I was totally a dick and did front on picking people up because so many people wanted to go racking, bombing, etc. It was just not possible to pick up everybody.

The BYI crew, who I was already really close with as well, had something RIS didn't at the time, girls, and parties and clubs and a broader sense of a NYC life for a kid that was not even a man yet, those things distracted me from bombing and racking so I started hanging out more with them. Chino was also one of my best friends now but couldn't bomb trains at the moment because he had a case with the vandal squad from the year earlier, he was laying low when it came to train graffiti.

I should add that I even acted like a dick towards Chino when a kid from my neighborhood that befriended him and followed him around started to have beef with me. I started bombing trains again in 1988 and didn't come around Chino and BYI as much for a couple months, that's when this kid from my neighborhood slipped in there.

One day this kid from my neighborhood went over a tag I had outside of Chino's girlfriend's house and Chino was with him, I never should have went over Chino but his girl's friend was also a girl I was kind of seeing or trying to see. My ego got the better of me and I not only went back over this kid from my neighborhood, I went over Chino outside his girl's house, and then I went to Brooklyn and went over a bunch of Chino throw ups in his own neighborhood. I was a total dick and I paid Chino back for that and I knew he was a true friend when he caught me and did not kick my ass but instead chose to talk through it. It was a funny war that went on for a couple months with him doing penis throw ups over me, but I'll let him tell that story, or maybe it will be in the sequel.

Needless to say, at this time I wasn't very popular, it was 1988 but I still had a homebase lay-up 57th. I was on the outs with RIS, but nothing was officially said, Ghost did go over one of my pieces Levitt's Field and I went back over him and he called me up and asked if we were going over each other now, a funny conversation to have on a telephone looking back. And now BYI was also going over me.

I was lean on partners at this time, so I bombed 57th often by myself. There were several writers that knew me that didn't want to get involved so even when I saw them in the lay-up, they would still do throw ups or pieces with me. But as far as friends I could count on there were only a few. Kite, Image, Cro, although Cro wasn't writing much at that time. Image was one of the few city writers that stood by my side throughout this.

Image and I met the previous year when Chino told me one Friday night to meet up at the foot of the Queens-boro Bridge on the Manhattan side because we were all going to hang out, it was a ton of writers there from uptown, Brooklyn, everywhere.

Some big-time train writers that I would bomb with used to tell me they don't come hang out like this because you never know what writers will be there and then everyone gets pictures of you and knows what you look like and it becomes a problem later.

We were meeting at 9pm and I got there a little early, already there was a group of about 20 writers there including uptown writers like Image, Arson, Vanal, and others.

They asked me what I wrote and when I told them, the writer Arson, who I hadn't ever met, got in my face and said I went over him at 175th on an A ridgie. I told him it definitely wasn't intentional and maybe it was just too dark at the back row where I did the throw up because often the police or other writers took out the lights. Sometimes it was so dark you couldn't see your hand in front of your face.

Arson was still in my face when Image said to him, "He said it was an accident, it's all good" and then Arson and I shook hands. Having just got out of that confrontation I turned and saw a tall white dude that was RD, I hadn't met him before. RD had beef with SP and Dash at the time and when Arson was confronting me, he said I did an "ST" over his throw up.

RD hears this and thinks he said "SP" and now thinks I am SP so he now gets in my face, and he was much bigger than I was so I started back peddling rather quickly as he was putting up his hands, I ran around some sort of obelisk or newsstand that is there on the 58th street corner to avoid getting hit just as I saw Chino walking up, I was like "Chino! You know RD?" and Chino asked what was going on and when RD told him it became apparent, I wasn't SP and it was done. This was a couple years before Chino and RD fought I believe, I wasn't there when that happened but I think it is detailed in another book.

Image and I, and Veefer would go on to become very good friends and Vice Presidents of each other's crews. Sounds silly now saying that but being VP of a crew back then was an honor and solidified your friendship. Image was one of the truest friends I ever had and if someone wanted to fight me, even if he didn't have beef with them, he took it as if they wanted to fight him and would immediately jump in front of me.

Anyway, back to the beginning of 1988, I was out of RIS in practicality but hadn't been told yet, I was hanging out with Image and Kite one afternoon when I spoke to another member of RIS that had just recently got down, he met Ghost through me but moved up the ranks very quickly. He asked if I wanted to do a piece at 57th tonight and to meet him there at midnight by the 61st street hatch.

Image and Kite wanted to do pieces also, so they came with me. We took the train to 5th Ave station on the N line, and walked up across from the Plaza hotel toward the 61st Street hatch, there was a payphone there on the corner where we all used to come up out of the lay-up sometimes to make calls, and meet writers there, etc.

As we walk up 5th Ave and get to about 60th street some older guy, like 8 years older than us runs up and jumps in my face. I had a backpack on and he immediately grabs one of the straps as if he is going to take my back pack. "What you write?" He says with his forehead pressed into my nose. If you have been in that situation where a guy is about to hit you know what I am talking about, they get so close and press right into you to intimidate.

"Stunc" I replied as I grabbed his wrist, "You're a fucking pussy!" He says. "Gimme your paint!".

I put both hands between me and him in a loose grapple to keep him from being able to swing up and hit me while he is still holding my bag. "You're fucking docked from RIS, now give me your paint!"

I half smile, by now Image, who carried an actual Louisville Slugger in a ¾ length goose down jacket, is taking the bat out and standing directly behind him. This guy is about to get hurt really fucking badly.

"You ain't getting my paint" I say as Image stands with the bat just waiting for the right moment, Kite is also moving in at this point, suddenly from across the street we hear "Noooooooooo!" as the writer that called me to meet him comes running to prevent this guy from getting hit. He gets in between us, and the older dude won't back down and keeps jawing at me. "Shut the fuck up and start walking" Kite tells him. The older dude responds "Go ahead you fucking bitches, go into the lay-up and paint, this is done". And he turns to walk off and leaves.

We find out who that was and it's still not clear if my friend that was setting me up knew what this guy's true intentions were or if the guy just told my friend that he wanted to talk to me.

So, the four of us now enter the lay-up through the vents near the central park zoo and we are walking down the new JFK Train tunnel to where it connects with the old N tunnels and the 57ths street tunnels.

But it's not over! Suddenly the sound of "being run up on" as running feet patter up from this older guy, now in the tunnel running towards me!

I pick up a pipe leaning against the wall and raise it, "You ain't going to do shit with that pipe because you're a bitch!" He screams, our voices now echoing in the tunnel, "Touch my bag and find out!" I screamed back. My friend that set this up gets in between again and cooler heads prevailed, the older guy wound up shaking my hand and telling me it was over. I took that as my exit from RIS and never put the crew up again.

The following week I was walking out of that same layup with my brother when Sane, Smith, this same older guy, and a few other RIS writers were walking in, I had a bag of scraps and they asked if I could leave them the "halvesies", I said "Sure but don't go over me in there." Joking but mostly serious, nothing worse than getting gone over with your own paint.

To my surprise, they did not go over me that night, even the guy that docked me from RIS, the respect is now mutual. Sane and Smith did go over one of my large throw-ups with their whole car, Smith tells the story in another book of how they saw me on the way in and tells how they had no choice but to go over one of my throw ups for their whole car, it's all good brother!

Chapter 11

THE STICK OUTS

In winter of 1986 I was on Main Street with Neo, Cro, and Gato and we were heading to our friend Sin's house at about 7 pm on a Friday night. Sin RIS was one of the best piecers we knew at the time, his letters were above and beyond and he was helping me with some outlines as we were all just writing in black books and doing sketches for our next pieces. We talked about going to do pieces one day soon on the 2s and 5s and decided we would definitely set that up the following week.

After a few hours, Cro and I wanted to go do a piece, so we left. We walked back from Sin's apartment on Northern Blvd. past Flushing High School and the YMCA and turned left toward Roosevelt and Main Street. We picked up cans at Cro's place on Kissena Blvd and then were trying to decide where to go do a piece, "Fuck it, let's go to Esplanade" says Cro.

Esplanade Tunnel and Stick-outs is one of the most famous lay-ups in New York and the home of MPC and where Seen and others did many famous cars through the years. It was two rows of 2s and 5s trains as far as the eye can see into the Morris Park Esplanade Tunnel and sticking out in the other direction.

You could write in either location, in the tunnel or on the stick outs but they were separated by a station and generally you stayed out of the station. I actually never painted in the tunnel there. The stick outs were a lot more inviting, the elevated tracks when they crossed

124

the streets were not all that high and they were on the ground for the most part except where they crossed the streets. I suppose this got higher and more elevated eventually, but to my recollection this is where I went several times.

Esplanade is essentially where we were all talking about going next week at Sin's just an hour earlier. Cro and I decide the best way for us to get there was to take the express city bus which leaves Main Street at 11pm to Tremont Ave. and then walk up from there into the Morris Park area. I've mentioned before, sometimes riding the train in to go write on trains can lead to detection by cops or running into other writers. Graffiti in general was a stealth mission and this was the best idea.

We got on the bus at Main Street near Roosevelt Ave. in front of what I think was "The Wiz" at the time. The bus makes three more stops down Main Street before making the left at Northern and getting on the highway for the express ride the rest of the way. At the second to last stop right near Norther Blvd, who do you think gets on the bus carrying bags of paint?

Neo, Gato, and Sin!

We were happy to see them, but they were not at all happy to see us. Specifically, me.

I was 16 years old at the time, the others all 18-20 years old, I was a newer writer and not someone that writers necessarily wanted to take with them on their missions, especially seasoned bombers and fighters that had beef with many writers and crews as I was a liability. I was someone that would need help but couldn't really provide help or carry my own weight. I get it, this sentiment was common in graffiti.

They knew exactly where we were going, and told us to get off the bus before it goes into the Bronx. "Fuck you, we're going" says Cro, adamantly. One of them picks up our bags and pushes open the bus window telling us he's going to drop the bags out and we better get off. Cro argues with them a little bit more and the guy holding our paint say "Fine" as he throws our bag back on the seat.

"When we get there, you guys walk your own direction and go into your own part of the lay-up, do not follow us". One of them said. "Good, fuck you guys" says Cro.

It's almost midnight when we get to East Tremont, we get off the bus and as agreed me and Cro walk in our own direction. The streets were quiet but not deserted, it wasn't all that late yet, people were still driving by and in front of their apartment buildings, corner stores, etc. We drew a few stares but for the most part the walk was uneventful.

It's always a bit strange walking through someone else's neighborhood to go into lay-ups, I mean imagine if you and your friends were hanging out on your street corner late at night and two guys you never saw came walking down your block with bags on their backs, dressed in army jackets? What would you think or do? A lot of times locals in these areas knew exactly why you were there, and they would give chase or try and start some problems or rob you. That thought was always on your mind.

We approached one of the overpasses in the Morris Park area, we could see the dark trains sitting above, we looked around there were no cars driving up, it was quiet, so we climbed onto the tracks. If you rode number trains at this time you would know that T-Kid and Vulcan were doing a lot of painting these days, they did a bunch of those cars at the Esplanade stick outs, and unsuspecting writers would "bring" them free paint when they wandered into the lay-up. We knew the stories.

Sure enough we get onto the tracks a look down about 100 yards and see three or four guys painting, they look down at us and start coming towards us, we knew exactly who it was and weren't ready to make a donation to their paint supply so we run down the tracks and cut through the train and down into the bushes on the other side.

Hiding in the bush with our hearts pounding we can hear their voices as they are looking for us and we hear their footsteps crunching as they stomp by. We are a long way from home, and outnumbered and outsized. This was a situation we could not win; our only option was to stay there until they went back to finish their car and then sneak out. Which is what we did.

We walked a few more overpasses towards Morris Park and found another way, about ¼ of a mile or so away from where those guys were and too far for them to see us. But when we get to this new location we hear a bunch a writers up on the tracks. At this exact moment, another coincidence in the amazing night, Gato, Neo and Sin walk up and see us.

"There's writers up there" says Cro. "I know, wait here." Says Gato as he climbs up into the layup alone. We hear some yelling and some banging then Gato comes back to where he can see us and says "Its ok, just some toys, come on."

It was unbelievable but that is exactly how it happened, no exaggeration. Cro and I did a "Stane Cro" window piece down on two side by side panels and Neo, Gato, Sin did a window down whole car on the next train. I painted the Stane outline Sin helped me with earlier that night at his apartment, I still have that little piece of paper today. The pic from that night is the cover of this book, Gato is making the peace sign above my head while covering his face from view.

Cro and I finished early and walked down all sides of the layup doing a bunch of throw ups each, I think we accidentally went over someone's piece and as a result our cars got dogged that night before they pulled out, my piece was the only one that survived because they didn't know who I was probably. Cope 2 went over the others but only put a line through mine. Kite eventually saw my piece running and took a picture for me at Times Square station.

See these photos and others on my @bronxscienceog Instagram page.

Chapter 12

ONE HUNDRED SEVENTY FIFTH

If you grew up in the city in the 1980s you remember certain neighborhoods and blocks was just always poppin', always hot, always some bullshit going down and for the most part you tried to avoid those blocks
.

One of the craziest things about graffiti is that it would lead you to these types of areas time and time again, and you might escape with your life or freedom on one night and go right back again not long after.

There were many lay-ups and yards that you did not want to get caught in, many that were run or overrun by locals looking to make a name for themselves, and in that sense few lay-ups rivaled 175th Street Lay-up on the A Train in the Washington Heights part of New York City in the mid-later 1980s.

Washington Heights was a largely Dominican neighborhood that lived in the shadow of the George Washington Bridge. In the 1980s this neighborhood in general was pretty wild and like Harlem to the South East, it was not really a great place to be wandering around lost if you weren't with anyone from the area.

It also happened to be a place where they parked ridgie C trains and A trains on the five tracks that filled an isolated cave beneath the streets of the city. It connected to the 1 train tunnel below and often to avoid detection we would arrive at the 168th street station on the 1 train and walk those tunnels in from there.

The lay-up held probably about 7 or more trains when fully packed including the lead in track but I never counted when I was there and am not entirely sure if that was the actual number, it just seemed like a small yard more than a lay-up.

During my time it was frequented by writers like Smith and Sane, Jon 156 and the 156 crew, Chris 217, Sand, and others as they were from that area. Those writers and crews for the most part were well known writers and you would rarely have any problems if it was them that you ran into in there. Also, they were writers that would sneak in and out of there like most other writers without hanging out and causing trouble.

But by 1986 it started to be overrun by a local crew that weren't as much into the art as the previously mentioned but more into the mischief and more into the street kid mentality. Many wanted to be stick up kids and hard rocks at the time. A bad combination for a neighborhood when you came to visit from the outside areas.

This was a crew called XX and was predominately kids that just happened to live above these trains and went into the lay-up to cause havoc. None of them really got up or had any other notable fame outside of these trains. But they did do some insides and minor damage on these trains with the paint they largely stole from unsuspecting writers.

There were only three of them that I even remember seeing up, but there was about 10 of them there on any given night. I think at one point almost every night it seemed they would wander down in there just to see what was going on and for many writers it became unfortunate if they happened to be there when they arrived. I was in that lay-up five times and three of those times they were there. Many years later I spoke with a writer from there that knew a lot of them and he told me the kids I knew from that crew went on to catch heavy cases and go to prison for almost lifetime bids. Not really all that surprising looking back.

They developed beef with some crews like CAC and others that would often run into them or go over them and in general they had little friends besides other uptown writers that might know them from the neighborhoods. They did link up with some other more respected writers from time to time and sometimes even these more respected writers would rob people and participate in the mayhem with them.

I'm not here to out any writers that either got hurt or did the hurting in any serious crimes, I will not be naming names in some of these stories and will change some of the names in the stories directly related to myself. Some of these events were serious crimes causing serious injuries, others more interesting, but all of them true.

There was a crew we hung out with in the village. They ventured up into 175th one night which they had done on occasion before. This night in particular the local crew of troublemakers was in there causing mayhem and they ran into them. The local XX crew was with another more famous uptown writer of ill repute when the trouble started and this uptown writer had what was commonly known as a "Rambo Knife" back then. A very dangerous 12" long blade with a saw on the back. It was called a Rambo knife because it was made famous in the First Blood movie a few years earlier.

This one writer wound up plunging that knife all the way into the chest of this downtown kid during the robbery and leaving him for dead. This downtown kid managed to survive and lived to tell that story.

In another incident that year, members of the 156 crew and a writer I was close with went into there and had similar trouble where someone hit him in the head with a sawed-off shotgun severing his ear from his head. That was right about the end of the line for that lay-up as a place to visit for writers not from there. The trains parked in there looked disgusting by then as well. Nothing but toys pretty much left covering everything inside and out with marker tags and shitty throw ups. No good looking graffiti left coming out of there.

One funny story from there involving Image KKB was

he had a brand-new pair of white sneakers on when he went, they were getting dirty so he took them off and put them in a paper bag and stashed them in the tunnel. He was walking around the lay-up in his socks when those local kids came in there. There was no immediate violence because Image and his boys were quite capable of violence themselves, but there was tension and they decided to leave. Someone found his sneakers apparently because they weren't where he thought he left them, or maybe he just couldn't remember exactly where he put them. He left the lay-up barefoot that night.

The first Time I went to that lay-up was with this kid Done FPV in 1986, we had heard about it and just went blind. Sure enough the XX crew did run up on us and they chased us out of the lay-up tunnel, they told us they were CAC and for a moment I believed them but later found out they only said that because they had beef with CAC. At the time I was carrying four cans in the sleeves of my army jacket and they thought I was empty handed looking for old cans in there and just chased us down the tunnel not realizing we had paint to take.

The second time I went back with Cro RIS and we entered from the 168th street tunnel on the 1 line. There were no trains parked in there and we ran into a writer from XX that was down there scouting it. He wrote BLAH (His real tag is not important) and was trying to befriend us but it was obvious he was only trying to stall until his boys arrived. We walked around the tunnels down there for about 20 minutes with this kid following us and inviting us to come back and bring paint and smash the yard telling us everything would be cool. But it was just too obvious what was happening. As we walked down one of the A tunnels, he got a little too close and Cro pulled out a knife as we climbed up onto the closed end of the A Station platform. He stuck the knife right near this kid's face and told him to back up and stop following us.

Back then there were no cell phones or means for that kid to communicate to his boys where we were, he could only hope that while we were wandering those tunnels, they would happen upon us and all rush us. It was super fucking creepy, and we left through the station and walked off into the night.

About 3 weeks later Cro and I went back there with Angel, this time we also entered in from the 1 tunnel on 168th street. But when we got up into the A tunnels, we could see the lay-up was packed with trains but that was all we could see. Every light in the tunnels was taken out, it was pitch black. Cops would sometimes take out all the lights in certain tunnels to discourage writers.

Sometimes stupid writers would just break the lights too, it was unclear as of yet what we were dealing with but we heard a bunch of voices further in the back that sounded like grown men, so we went towards the A Tunnel hatch to go upstairs back to the street.

All the lights were off in this corridor and staircase. There was a complete absence of light, so dark you could not see your hand in front of your face. We were quite literally blind and walked by holding onto the wall up the stairs.

As we pushed the hatch open someone from the street

134

side pulled it up and it was uniform police shining a flashlights down at us. In complete panic and surprise, we fell backwards down the stairs and took off running back into the lay-up with those cops behind us in the hatch and radioing to the plain clothes officers that were already in the lay-up. Apparently, a huge raid just took place and if we arrived from the street side, we would have known this because we would have seen all of the transit police vehicles but because we came over through the 1 tunnel, we had no idea.

Once back in the lay-up we could see the flashlights running down the tracks towards us and we ran down the floater platform along the wall of the first parked train, about midway Cro slipped in between cars of the dark train and climbed up onto the top of the train, then I followed and was laying on my belly between the train roof and the tunnel top when Angel climbed up and didn't have enough room. He shoved me to move me over and I slide off the train down onto the side with no platform which is about a 10-foot drop landing on the tracks below.

I screamed as the horror of that unfolded, and the cops, now on the floater platform right near where we were hiding on top of the train heard this and shined the lights up at them, they dropped down next to me and we hauled ass between two rows of trains all the way out the front or back of the lay-up, I'm not even sure which way we wound up because we were north of the 175th street station now and when we popped out of the hatch exit we were in a park under the George Washington Bridge. It was a long run past those trains through the tunnel, I was having trouble keeping up as I had a medical condition and I kept calling out to them to wait for me, which they did but they kept pushing me forward.

Once in the park we ran further down into the trees under the bridge and just hid out for about 30 minutes before making our way back towards downtown.

About a month or so after that I went back with Cro RIS and an older ALLCITY writer with a reputation for being a fighter. We will call this writer ALLCITY for the sake of this story.

We were going to sneak in from the 1 train tunnel as usual, but ALLCITY said he wanted to take the train straight into the 175th street station so he could see what was going on rather than walk in blind from the one tunnel to a packed lay-up. It was late, about 1am on a weeknight now so I guess it made sense. Normally as I mention you didn't want to enter through a lay-up station but in this case the station was pretty big and was not immediately adjacent to the lay-up trains, so it wasn't as big of a deal.

We rode the train in with huge bags of paint on our backs, we had about 10 cans each and planned on crushing the entire lay-up that night.

We got off the train and the station seemed deserted at first, the trains left and as we walked towards the tunnel end of the platform we could see a group of kids.

Oh fuck! I immediately thought to myself.

Between them and us was a staircase that went up to a

closed down part of the station that was exit only after certain hours, and there was the tunnel in the other direction behind us.

"Let's go out this other tunnel." Said Cro, I quickly agreed.

"Nah, hold on a sec," said ALLCITY as he started to walk up the staircase to the closed part of the station an exit. We followed. When we got up the stairs, we could see these kids now coming up the other staircases into this part of the station because they saw us.

"Let's run" I said.

"We ain't running" said ALLCITY who picked up something off the floor to use as a weapon in case it popped off.

The group ran up on us.

"What you write?!" the first kid exclaimed as he got into ALLCITY's face and took a swing. ALLCITY swung back and BAM! Down he went when ALLCITY hit him, and it was on! Everyone was fighting. Us three against ten to twelve of them.

I was wearing an Adidas track jacket this night, something I wore often to lay-ups and in the pocket, I always kept Halt which was a form of mace, or more specifically dog repellent that mail carriers would keep clipped to their carts. Kids would steal these when they went up to deliver the mail.

I pulled it out and sprayed three guys that were coming at me, I threw a punch at one as the other punched me in the side of the head sending me forward.

I tumbled onto the ground and jumped back up continuing to spray the mace. It got knocked out of my hand in the melee and they were pulling my bag off my back.

"Get the bag!" one of them exclaimed.

At this point I had no idea what was happening with my two friends because it was chaos and screaming and I was fighting for my life. As my bag came off, I wrestled it free and swung the heavy bag around into one of them that had been maced knocking him to the floor. Almost instantly I got knocked over by a few of them and they started to stomp on me and kick me so I curled up in a ball just lying there being beaten.

In a flash of realization, my two friends must be either dead or gone now because all ten of these guys were kicking me and one climbed on top of me and grabbed me by the hair and started smashing my head into the concrete of the station floor.

"I want to see you bleed!" he screamed.

I was just about unconscious when a bloody figure reappeared, it was ALLCITY who came back for me and started throwing people to the floor and smashing people like Thor with a pipe he now had found.

He picked me up and screamed into my face RUN! As

he pushed me up the stairs with the group of locals still swinging on us and trying to stop us. He kept fighting them off as we got out of the station onto the street and he screamed at me to run again and I did, right down the middle of the street as fast as I could, I only had half a shirt on at this point and was covered in blood and there were three of them chasing me. ALLCITY must have went a different direction or gotten killed because it was just me running for my life now with these three in pursuit.

I came to Broadway and just made a right and was running down the middle of the street, a complete mess of a 17-year-old kid. I can only imagine how bad it looked because a yellow New York City Taxi pulled up with a couple in the back, they threw open the door and told me to jump in and I did.

They were gasping in horror and asking the taxi driver to radio for the police. He told me he was taking me to times square and I can get to the police there. I looked back out the rear window at the three that were chasing me, and I could barely see them now. Struggling to catch my breath I sunk back into the seat as the woman looked at me with compassion and sorrow in her eyes. I closed mine.

Barely conscious they woke me up as the taxi was dropping me off in Times Square, they point to the police and told me to go over to them and have them call an ambulance.

I did not go to the police or hospital, I just wanted to get home. My dad can take me to the hospital when I get back.

I staggered into the times square station, a gash inside my mouth would need stitches and was gushing blood down my throat, I had three broken ribs and one eye swollen shut. By now it's about 4am and trains are starting to get a little busier again as people start coming in early for the next day. I was sitting on the stairs half asleep waiting for the 7 train when some woman looked at me and said, "You're disgusting, look at yourself!"

She obviously thought I was a junkie or prostitute or something. I paid her little mind and when the train came, I got on.

I sat on the 7 train out to Main Street which grew more crowded as the time got closer to 5am. At 74th and Broadway in Queens people got on transferring from the letter lines. A person covered in blood with no shirt on immediately caught my eye, he had his shirt held up against a gushing stab wound on the back of his neck, it was ALLCITY who saw me and came and dropped on the seat next to me exhausted.

Commuters on the train moved away in horror at the sight of the two of us. He looked over at me, battered and bloody.

"Stane, welcome to the wonderful world of graffiti... I fucking quit." He said.

Chapter 13

NEW SNOW

New snow was always a magical thing in NYC growing up in the 80's, probably still is but I am not there anymore to enjoy it.

By the 1990's new snow meant getting in my dad's jeep and leaving my house and driving directly into the park across the street and using parks and sidewalks and anything else, as extensions of the street. New snow basically gave us license to drive anyway and any how we saw fit. Police at that time in New York City did not have 4 wheel drive vehicles, so they wouldn't even bother, they didn't even have front wheel drive vehicles, for the most part they were still rolling the 1980s Caprice Classics.

Snow also meant donuts, AKA recklessly driving out of control in sliding circles, and some of the first were always done in the Golden Field parking lot, in front of the tall obelisk of a Vietnam memorial, large, open, nothing to crash into. At least that's what my friend Trent thought when he picked us up one night in his dad's 1988 Ford Thunderbird 5.0 with the Mustang engine. It was rear wheel drive on 50's (A term used for lower profile racing tires that had awful traction to begin with), it was impossible to drive anywhere in the snow without the wheels spinning endlessly in this thing.

My brother was in the front seat and Jimmy and myself were in the back. The joyride ensued eventually ending with a slam against what Trent thought was the curb which rendered the vehicle barely drivable.
"I think I cracked a rim" is what he said specifically.

My brother put the window down and stuck his head out and said "Holy shit this thing is totaled!"

Trent hit more than the curb, well, the curb first, then the momentum and centrifugal G forces carried the body into an electrical pole, largely with the help of the suspension.

The car was indeed almost totaled, we kicked the metal and tugged on it and eventually it could drive but the frame was clearly bent and the car had a hint of a U Shape, and the passenger side smashed in completely.

Trent's, and our, first instinct was that for insurance and parental purposes we needed to make this look like a legitimate accident, as the car being in the closed park in the middle of the night was clearly an indication of tomfoolery.

We took it about a half mile away to Bell Blvd, near Bay Terrace shopping center and tried to slide it into a pole on a legitimate street corner, recreating the accident to look like it was an honest loss of control on a turn due to the snow. But we couldn't quite get it close enough to a pole, we got out, we were trying to push the car into a position that looked believable, ultimately giving up and going to plan B.

Plan B? Yes, there was a plan B, and in our town, everyone's plan B was "report the car stolen". It was a neighborhood ritual and often done although we had never done it yet.

But surely how could we call the police and make this believable? It was almost midnight now on a Thursday night, in the snow on nearly abandoned streets. And this car in particular would be the last target for thieves in this weather.

We came up with a plan, five years before Scorsese would release Goodfellas, we decided to have Trent and my brother eat at the local diner, order a meal, while Jimmy and I got rid of the car. We dropped them off, when they were done, they would pay the check, then walk out to the parking lot as if they had a car before running back in and declaring "My car has been stolen!" and having the diner call the police.

Jimmy and I took the car from there, on a bit of a joy-ride, because why not? It wasn't stolen yet, but it was about to be reported so in 30 minutes or less. We beat the hell out of it with punk rock music blasting. Specifically, SNFU and at the point their song "This is the end" came on the night was in full bloom.

Before too long however, we went and picked up Jimmy's car so he could follow me to some apartments near Fresh Meadows Queens which would be this thing's final destination. Upon arrival I careened up onto the sidewalk and right through a glass bus stop enclosure sending bits of shattered safety glass everywhere, and adding a bit more damage to the car.

I kind of did it on purpose assuming it would just hit the enclosure and look believable, but the snow underneath was icing over by now and the rate of speed seemed to increase in the slide causing a much more dramatic smash through than I originally intended. But hey, it was all part of the show at this point.

Then I went to work on the steering column and radio with a screwdriver, cracking plastic everywhere and snipping wires, all to add the illusion of foul play and theft.

Ironically the car was almost totaled, but not quite, and the insurance company notified Trent's dad about a week later that the car had been "recovered" and that it was just under the threshold for totaling, meaning that they would make the repairs and return this black eye to him and his family.

Trent had to live with the lies and the guilt for the next year or more knowing the true fate of his family's car, an ironic but probably well-deserved punishment and a small price to pay in retrospect.

The reality is however, Trent, and all of us, had a history of transgressions with our parents cars, but Trent's seemed the funniest for some reason.

His dad owned a Pontiac Fiero in the years prior to this, if you are not familiar with the Fiero, it was Pontiac's, very lame attempt at a two-seater Ferrari looking car that would sell for about 1/10th the cost.

Trent's dad's was a 5 speed manual, and this is where I would learn to drive 5 speed at 15 years old, unlicensed and without our parent's permission at night in the streets while they all slept. Incidentally the concept of a clutch was already very familiar to us from years of having ridden dirt bikes and other strangely acquired vehicles throughout our neighborhoods and parks.

One particularly cold night Trent worked the Fiero up to some significant speed down a side street eating a stop sign across the main road, in this case maybe 221st street. The slope of the main road for drainage made it a huge hump as it crossed the side streets, and hit at speed it sent us airborne, probably only about 20" above the ground, but airborne in a car is airborne none the less.

Upon touching back down, the force of the impact caused stress cracks in the center of the car's spoilers, and door panels, an indication that the frame flexed and probably caused significant underlying damage. But we laughed and at the end of the night that car went back in the garage, smelling of burnt clutch and rubber, and his parents were none the wiser.

A couple of years later when his mom got a brand new Chrysler Lebaron, champagne colored inside and out, Trent took that out, 2 days old, and threw it into park deliberately at 40 miles per hour for no reason other than to hear the park stop buzz like a roulette wheel. I'll never forget the hilarity of that moment, stupid now looking back, but we still laugh about this to this day, almost 40 years later.

How did we possibly get to this point? Where we had no regard for the laws of the city nor the law of our households? What I have detailed so far isn't even the tip of the iceberg of what we perpetrated against society, but we were seemingly good kids, from seemingly great families with no reason to have so much angst and outward disrespect for the outside world.

We got heavily into punk rock by 1982 and hardcore soon after, we dropped in and out of high school/s, being kicked out of some, but all eventually graduating, which in NYC at that time was no hard feat. If you had even close to enough credits they would eventually just tell you to take a diploma and leave, I suppose to keep their numbers up with kids that were even "Close enough" as opposed to the so many that couldn't even get close.

But the punk rock and hardcore was not the cause of this either, it was also a result of what led us here, it was the result of the times, and absentee parents during the

146

day who were working, it was the direct result of bad economies and lack of things to do at home, inferior technology and more.

Paths, and rights of passage in the town where we lived, but mostly just literal paths led us here. Paths beaten into the grass and weeds, and bushes through parts of the city and parks where people weren't supposed to travel. Paths that led to an under society and exposure to things seemingly nonexistent in most lower middle class neighborhoods. Exposure to things we never should have seen or saw on a daily basis as 10 year olds, and 11 year olds and so on. Things that would become ingrained in our conscious and lead us exactly where society did not want us being led.

In the 1980's new snow meant trains were parked in tunnels more than normally, because train yards being outside were not ideal in blizzard situations. They used to line express tracks in tunnels on many lines with trains parked overnight whenever it would snow and it would create opportunities to bomb more trains in one spot than would normally be there otherwise. One particular run of layups was around the 28th street stations on the then R line in Manhattan, these layups would stretch station after station under certain conditions where they might not otherwise be there.

Another bonus of newly falling snow is the streets would be largely empty of normal citizens and even the police would rarely be out. It created a very serene quiet setting for which you could be alone with your thoughts and paint and do things in almost complete silence that would otherwise be marred by traffic noise, too many people, police, and more.

One of these joys was handball courts, if you went to piece on a handball court while it was snowing it was dead silent and you would hear the sound of the snow crunching under your feet. Walls that commonly were very dark now had additional illumination reflected up on them by the white blanket beneath. It was just such a great memory.

Chapter 14

NEVER HEARD OF YOU

I graduated college finally in the late 1990s and my brother had already been living in Los Angeles for a year at that point. Having been going back and forth to stay with him I decided that after all I had been through and mentally wanting something completely new I would move out to Los Angeles to start a new life with three or four other true New Yorkers, and we did.

In my final weeks Chino was working at a bar downtown near Tribeca called Senor Teddy's and the old school writer Erni Paze was also moving out to Los Angeles the same week I did. They were having a bit of a going away get together for him and Chino invited me down as it was fitting for me too.

Growing up JSON and CAP were legendary in the very early 80s. I remember them from 'the book' and from expressways driving in my dad's car up in the Bronx where he was from. It seemed my dad was always heading into the Bronx for some reason, whether it was to Arthur Ave or taking me to the Bronx Zoo, I was also starting Bronx Science soon.

I had met Cap in late 1986 at the bakery where he worked nights near Morris Park.

Neo was fairly close to him and used to go hang out with him often, Med and Fayde were working at Waldbaums in Bayside at the time on Francis Lewis Blvd along with Neo, so I met them there. This was the time

Med and Fayde started crushing some pretty tough spots around the Bayside area, doing things like pulling their car up onto the sidewalk and standing on the roof to do high straight letters, things that hadn't been done before.

In 1987 Neo told me I was down with MPC and to start putting it up but I would never put up a crew if I wasn't put down by the originators, the idea of being recruited or told to put it up by an extended party just never made sense to me. I told Neo that and he said fine, let's go up to the Bronx and hang out with Cap and then he can tell you you're down, so we did.

We drove up to the bakery where Cap worked the night shift, he came out and hung out with us for about half an hour, he told me I was down and that the crew currently had beef with Cope 2 so that meant I should cross out Cope 2 when I see him up, he was serious but also I sensed he was partially joking. But the more I think about it now, he was probably serious.

I agreed and that's when I started putting up MPC. Incidentally Cope did cross out a piece I did on the 5s in early 1987 with just a single line through it, I did not come across any of his throw ups on the 5s at that time because he was already getting smashed by MPC and I did not ever see any of it when I was in the Esplanade layups the two or three times I went.

But by 1998, I still had never met Json, until this night at Senor Teddys.

It was a weird thing when you met a legendary writer sometimes and they asked what you write, not in a confrontational way but just socially. Even now removed from Graffiti all the way to 1998 that feeling was still there. If someone asks what you write and they haven't heard of you, if they are polite, they will say something like "Oh ok cool." And move on in the conversation. If they want to be a dick, the biggest insult you can say to another writer in that situation is to reply, "Never heard of you."

That would literally be the equivalent of being introduced to someone at a dinner party and them asking what you did for a living and when you told them they said "Oh, that's whack."

So much so in fact that huge graffiti wars have started over that exact incident, more than one. One example would be back in 1984ish Ghost met Revolt and several other RTW writers at a gallery show in lower Manhattan. One of them asked Ghost what he wrote and when he told them they replied, "Never heard of you."

That night Ghost went to the City Hall layup and went over everyone he saw up in RTW, writing inside of his throw ups "Heard of me now?" and that's how RIS wound up having beef through the 1980s with the RTW crew. At least that's what they told me when I became part of the crew in late 1986.

So when Chino introduced me to Json, it was indeed that moment, Chino introduced me as Chris, but Json as Json Terror, Json responded as he shook my hand, "Whassup, what do you write?" Not wanting to risk that situation I described above, I responded "You wouldn't have heard of me" figuring that he never rode the letter lines in the years I was active and there's no point in having this conversation.

"Try me" he said, wanting to know what I wrote, so I told him Stane, and he quickly responded, "Stane and Droma."

What I didn't realize is, that regardless of whether he rode the letter lines much when I was active, he did take the bridges into Queens regularly and me and my brother smashed all of those local highways, so he did see me up.

What a relief.

Silly though, isn't it? Three years at this point since I had written my name on anything or did a piece and even after my college graduation and starting my new life, I was concerned about a writer not having heard of me.

It's one of those things that comes with the compulsion of Graffiti, if you never really did it you will never understand those little nuances, but if you did dedicate your life to it at one point, even in your childhood, those little nuances will still matter even when you are a senior citizen.

And that's just the way it is.

Chapter 15

COLD WAR BOYS

The 1980s was the end of the cold war, it was real and tangible in our lives. There were air raid sirens on occasion and fallout shelter icons on most major buildings with a basement level. The fallout shelter signs were a three-triangle radioactive symbol painted black on a bright yellow metal, it was a reminder what the cold war meant, potential nuclear destruction.

Ask kids we didn't really care all that much about it, or the sirens, but our parents did. My mom would watch the news often and obsess over the idea that "World War III" was going to start. We had HBO at the time, it has been around that long. But HBO wasn't cable in New York City, it was its own box that sat on top of your TV and offered only HBO, which was a limited channel that showed occasional movies. It was basically a subscription service to a cable type box that offered only one more channel to your TV which had about 11 working stations at the time.

HBO's only competitor in New York City, where cable television was not yet available, was WHT, Whomecto Home Theater. Or something like that, I am sure I spelled it wrong but it's not even worth a google search for me now because it is neither here nor there in the story. It was also one station and late at night they used to offer porn which you could not see without making some sort of payment for a single view or something. Anyway, we had one of those, or both but at different times.

I think to activate it you had to put your TV on channel 3 or something and then turn it on. One morning I was in the shower, and I guess HBO was left on from the night before. I was a very young boy, probably in 1984 or something. My mom turned on the TV not realizing a movie would be playing and it was a movie where they had a newscast at that moment discussing missiles that had been launched at the United States by Russia, maybe it was Wargames? I never found out what movie for sure. But my mom lost it, she thought it was real news and kicked in my bathroom door and dropped to the ground hysterical, World War III was starting in her mind.

As I mentioned, racism in New York at this time was prevalent, it wasn't necessarily like a dirty south kind of racism where the klan might show up but there were occasional news stories of racist attacks in Howard Beach or Bensonhurst Brooklyn, heavily Italian neighborhoods that did not have the best relationships with African Americans or Latinos. If you have ever watched a Spike Lee movie you know what I mean.

Mostly though New York at this time was heavily segregated, not by any sort of political doing or laws but by immigrants largely settling where other immigrants from their country settled during the early part of the 20th century, and economics also pushed certain groups together into public housing and things like that.

Growing up in New York and as a storyteller, it was and is common to use descriptors when talking about someone, by today's standards they might seem a little off and my wife gives me shit about it until this day. Like if you got rushed by four Spanish dudes you would tell the story as I got rushed by four Spanish dudes, or if it was four Black guys you would say four Black guys, or even if they were white you would say four white guys. You really can't tell a story without telling the descriptors of what everyone looks like.

The other day I had an interaction with a girl on an elevator and it was very pleasantly inspiring, not about race or anything to do but the girl happened to be black, so when I told the story to my wife I said "this black girl got on the elevator ..." because to me that was the natural description of setting the scene. My wife immediately corrects me saying "Why do you need to tell me her race?" and the answer is I don't and I don't know, but I would have said the same thing if it was a white girl, Italian girl, or Asian, etc. It just sets the scene visually for me in the story, and as someone that has had several screenplays optioned by major Hollywood studios it is industry standard to describe the characters by age, race, sex, etc. each time a new character is introduced. Even if it really doesn't have anything to do with the story.

Otherwise, it is like that Seinfeld episode where George tries to pretend he has a black friend and hires an exterminator to come to dinner. Then later someone asks George "Oh you mean the black guy?" and George says "Hmmmm. You know, I don't really see people in ways of color but now that you mention it, I think he is black." Or something like that, I am paraphrasing a bit, but you get the idea.

I think it is human nature to describe people by what

you see and our differences without being fueled by prejudice or hate. That's not to say there wasn't plenty of hate to go around, but just not every description of someone as a black guy or a white boy was fueled by hate, sometimes it just fit.

Today I see old Mike Tyson clips all of the time on IG Stories and Tik Tok and he often calls out adversaries in the audience as "White boy". And people on IG or TikTok start going on about how racist that is and how Mike is racist. But growing up where and when Mike grew up, like many of us, it just simply was not really racist, it was just part of life to describe other people the way you saw them.

One day when we were young my dad overheard some kids in our group saying some stuff about kids from that side of the park, with Gibson present, insulting things. Again, I mention some of the things Gibson had to hear in another one of these stories. But either way my dad figured it was time to have a talk with me and my brother about racism in this country, this was in 1983 or so and we were like 11 or 12 years old at the time.

My dad came from Italy with his parents and brother right when he was born, and they came through Ellis Island and settled in the Bronx, not far from Fordham Road I think, my dad went to Evander Childs High School in Gun Hill. His brother, my uncle, was also a published writer and he tells some interesting stories of racial integration parts of the Bronx that went from heavily Italian to African American, one of them published in a New York newspaper.

Upon graduation from High School, like literally the day he graduated, my dad was handed a draft notice from the Marines that he was going to fight in the Korean War. What a graduation present huh?

Off my dad went to bootcamp on Parris Island, off to Korea, awful war stories and the whole nine yards. After two years he was honorably discharged and stationed back in Washington D.C. the capital of the United States, while he transitioned out of the military and back into civilian life. One of his better friends from the Korean station of the war was a black guy that was a huge boxing fan just like my dad. This was right around 1953 or so in the United States, in Washington D.C..

I keep repeating where and when because it is going to be hard to believe as I tell this story, and this was not in some backwards southern town waving confederate flags, it was in our capital. To put this into even more perspective this happened thirty years prior to my dad telling me this story, the equivalent of something that happened in 1993 in my book. 1993 feels like yesterday to me, and 1953 felt like yesterday to my dad then.

They were huge fight fans but they each liked a different fighter of a highly anticipated upcoming bout. Like many people in the military, they would bet and gamble with each other and they had a huge wager on the outcome of the fight, and they would really go at it about who's guy was better. I can't remember who was fighting anymore.

At the time in 1953, movie theaters would bring in live sporting events and you would buy a ticket and it was the PPV of the time, but only the theaters could receive that PPV signal as technology wasn't there yet that you could watch it at home, or even have a TV for most people. It was either you go there and watch it live or listen on the radio.

My dad and his friend were working out, talking shit to each other about the fight the night before. At the end of the workout my dad says, "I'll pick you up at seven tomorrow."

"For what?" His friend replies.

"For the fight" my dad says.

The guy tells my dad he isn't going, my dad starts really getting on his case about being a chicken shit that his guy will lose, and he better have the money, etc. The guy finally interrupts my dad –

"Look! I'm not allowed in that theater!"

My dad tells me he literally almost fell over in disbelief and disgust when he heard that, he did not understand, but sure enough in Washington mother fucking D.C., in the United States, A Marine who was black that just fought for his country, was not allowed into a movie theater because of the color of his skin.

My dad goes on to explain that Gibson's father who was my dad's age, and all of those other kid's fathers that were his age, how the fuck could they have the same opportunity as me when their dads were not allowed to go to the same stores as my dad, they could not attend the same schools, they couldn't even go into a fucking movie theater in Washington D.C. after the Korean war. And this largely continued until about 1960, which again, in perspective is about the year 2000 from the time this book was written.

That story blew me away, and while I truly feel that we all have the same opportunities going forward, I think our fathers had vastly different opportunities, and those opportunities helped certain fathers get their kids raised into the right areas and economic situations and in my opinion the true barrier to equal opportunity today is not the color of your skin but the economic situation from where you start. We may all have equal opportunities going forward but we don't all have the same starting line to reach our goals.

This is the part of the book that probably falls under unsolicited opinion, but here it is anyway.

I see it all of the time on Twitter and IG, people saying things like "If I said I was proud to be white I'd be called a racist" and other things like that. "If we had a White Entertainment Television …." and so on.

There was a show called "All In the Family" that was about an extremely uneducated racist man named Archie Bunker. Archie was played by a school teacher and theater actor named Carrol O'Conner and he was a brilliant man. The show was often misunderstood as a racist show rather than the satire it was highlighting the ignorance of the common bigot. It was filmed in front of a studio audience and some of the biggest names in Hollywood were involved and/or on the show, it spun off several amazing shows like Good Times, The Jeffersons, and others. Carrol would go on to win two NAACP awards for his work on his following show that also dealt with racism. He won five Grammys I believe as well.

There is an episode on All In The Family where Archie is having his refrigerator repaired by a white repairman that has a black helper. Archie is uncomfortable with the black guy in his house and starts jawing at him, they get into a heated discussion that culminates with the black guy saying "Hey! I'm proud to be black!"

Archie replies "Ok, ok, calm down, I'm proud to be white but you don't hear me making a federal case about it."

The black guy replies "That's because you never had to!"

End Scene.

"Making a federal case out of it" was a common idiom used in the 60s thru the 80s and meant to make a big deal out of something.

But the truth in that statement was beautifully depicted. White people can't say things like "White Pride" without being deemed racist because they never had a time where they were mistreated because of their skin color. Black people can say "Black pride" without being deemed racists because they have had the opposite experience in this country historically and they needed to stand up and say that out loud.

One could argue, and they have, and they'd be right, that many white groups have faced racism and mistreatment over time, such as the Italians and Irish when they first came to the United States, and in that context you could indeed proclaim you are proud to be Italian or proud to be Irish without being considered racist at all.

Because those are nationalities and not ethnicities, and there are indeed people of all colors that have been born and raised in Italy and Ireland that are proud citizens of those nations and not in the slightest way white.

It was a warming moment for me as a father when I overheard my son, a proud first generation Italian American on his Mother's side, proclaim with excitement to one of his friends that Khaby Lame, the TikTok superstar was Italian. My son has been spared a lot of the generational preconceived notions about people and views the world in a much more innocent way. And at 9 years old he already knows that a person of any nationality can be any race.

CRAZY WHITE BOYS

There was a Woolworth at the corner of Main Street and Roosevelt Ave. in Flushing Queens in the 1980s that was probably there since the 40s or 50s. As far as I know it is long gone now. In 1984 when I was about 13 years old I went into that Woolworth with a kid that wrote Taro.

He had become friends with the writer Sin RIS by then who worked in Pearl Paint or whatever equivalent art store was there on Main Street a few blocks further towards Northern Blvd., and Taro's black books and pieces today would still burn better than 90% of other graffiti. He was extremely talented and made connections with CAC and Sin very early on because of it.

Because of that connection we found ourselves on Main Street and in Woolworth racking. We had bookbags, which is really one of the worst ways to rack because it is so obvious. We put about 4 Krylons each in the bags and walked out. As we stepped out the door they yelled to us from the store to stop because they knew we were stealing the paint.

In a panic we ran out the door and they started to chase us. Taro ran up Roosevelt away from Main Street and I ran across Main Street towards Shea Stadium.

About a block or two towards Shea Stadium on Roosevelt Ave. there was a public housing project known as "The Bland." They had a reputation of being a bit dangerous at the time and if you have no clue what I am talking about this is an example of what was commonly referred to as "The Projects" in popular culture when talking about inner city housing and youth.

I was still running from the guy at Woolworth's in my mind although he probably stopped running after me about a block ago, or never even crossed Main Street to begin with. But when you are a kid and when you are being chased it feels like the FBI and everyone is after you so you run and run thinking you are this huge criminal even though probably no one really cared that much.

I hook a left turn into "The Bland" and as I run through

the yard in between the buildings I throw my bookbag into some bushes and keep running across.

The buildings at this time were a spot for copping dope and the dudes selling it stand in front of different buildings, similar to what you would see in a show like The Wire.

They see me come running in here, throwing the bag and running across and obviously assume I am being chased by the cops. One of them runs out to Roosevelt Ave. to look around to see who is coming, they don't see anyone. By now I am behind the last building looking back across and one of them yells out to me.

"Yo!" he said. As another grabs my bag and walks towards me. He hears the rattling from the paint and opens the bag looking in then pushed the bag into my chest.

"I don't know what the fuck you're up to, but whatever the fuck you're doing do it someplace else because we don't need no fucking crazy white boy bringing the cops in here!"

Obviously, they were pissed because this is where they were doing business and I was bringing heat their way potentially. Makes sense to me looking back, and at the time I knew I was lucky that they really just wanted me out of there as quickly as possible and didn't fuck me up.

And that's sort of how New York was at the time. Each neighborhood had its own ethnicity, and many times the neighborhoods where we went to paint and to write on trains were not white neighborhoods and we stood out. Often times they referred to some of us as white boys.

Then it became something cool to put in my throw up, "Crazy White Boys". Then it became our crew, which incidentally had many members that were not white. And the initials CWB had many alternative meanings too, Cold Weather Bombers, Crazy Wicked Beatdowns, Cold War Brothers, and so on.

Chapter 16

WHERE I WAS WHEN

There are certain events in your lifetime that you will always remember where you were when they happened. In my dad's generation, Kennedy being assassinated was one of them.

There have been three for me, the towers falling on 9/11, Michael Jackson Dying (Oddly enough I was on a tee box at a golf course in Glendale), but the first one of these for me, is where I was when I heard Mike Tyson lost to Buster Douglas in 1990.

In the later 1980s there was a pool hall down a side street off of Bell Blvd. towards "The trestle", in Bayside Queens. It was a typical pool hall that attracted everything from thugs, drug dealers, gamblers, troublemakers, and normal people hanging out with friends. There were often incidents there, but it was part of the neighborhood and was someplace we went regularly.

I was exactly walking out of that pool hall holding the door for two guys that were squeezing in around me when I overheard one of them say to the other "Did you see the look on that cop's face when I told him Tyson lost?"

Ummmm what?

Before I can tell anymore of this story you first need to understand what Mike Tyson was in the 1980s in boxing and sports in general. He was the biggest sports superstar in the world, he was unstoppable, his athletic dominance was overshadowed only by his arrogance and perceived stupidity in pre and post fight interviews.

I grew to hate him just because he was one of those things that could not be beaten, and he knew it. Similarly, many years later, as a New York sports fan I always loathed Tom Brady, but as an adult now I can recognize greatness when I see it and love Brady as the best quarterback to ever play the game. In that same way, I love Tyson as the greatest brawler and fighter of my lifetime, and also respect the person and philosopher Mike has become through his adversity.

My dad used to have Tyson fight parties, he had a large screen television, and when I was a teen he would have a bunch of guys over, get a six foot hero, and bring the fight in on PPV. Tyson was so dominant it was annoying because the fights would often never make it past the first round and the nights would end early and as a kid back then having company over the house was exciting as there wasn't much to do once everyone left. It just felt empty. So Tyson went on to symbolize that emptiness to me as I got older and I hated him.

Now when I overheard the guy say that Tyson lost, my first thought was that he was full of shit. But there was no instant news in 1990, no looking at google or your phone, no 24 hour news networks, no place to actually check on anything, especially at 1 am at night. All you could do was ask someone you trusted that might know.

I ran to a payphone and called my father because I knew he was watching the fight with his friends that night and he would know.

"Can you fucking believe it" he said into the phone randomly as he answered. He knew it was me, he knew exactly why I was going to be calling.

Mike Tyson got too big for his own ego, he became undisciplined and fought a fighter that had nothing to lose and everything to gain, a fighter who just lost his mother and in the words of Eminem years later had his one shot and was going to capture everything he ever wanted in that moment.

Buster fought the fight of his life, he never looked that good before or after, his career would be short. Tyson fought a shitty fight and was unprepared, he no longer took his craft seriously now that he believed his own hype.

I just could not believe it. I went back to the pool hall and would tell each of my friends as they arrived, the ones that had no idea did not believe me, it was actually unbelievable in the truest sense of the word.

That night a brawl would break out in the pool hall between my friends and a group that came with a flushing writer called "Darkstar". I kind of knew it was going to pop off that night the second he walked in. Darkstar stood out as someone not from the neighborhood, he was tall, in an army jacket (which we no longer were wearing by 1990), had longer hair and a bearded goatee much thicker than most locals. He was with some of his boys that were from the Bayside area and friends with some of us, and my girl knew them from school too.

One kid was Bobbie DeKamp.

Something happened where my friend Chevy started swinging on him and during the brawl another kid I know broke a pool cue across Darkstar's back. The brawl didn't last long which is often the case, it was like a quick 30 seconds of chaos and glass shattering and then the group was out the door and our night resumed.

That night reminds me though of something I have talked about before and the worst-case scenario of such. That kid Bobbie DeKamp wound up getting "caught up" in another situation with "Darkstar" that had tragic results. And it is a story I tell to my son today to carefully choose the company you keep and how important it is that he control the situations he allows himself to get involved in or even just be there for. Just so my boy doesn't get "Caught up" and ruin his life.

The following year or so, Darkstar and Bobbie, and a group of others were in Manhattan going to the club Roseland. Like many knuckleheads of the day, Darkstar was a bit of a stick-up kid and would rob innocent people for money on nights they would go out. The reason I specify "innocent" people is because they are what cops call true victims.

Some hard rock stick-up kids wouldn't rob innocent people, instead they would rob other hard rocks or street kids, in the ultimate flex of strength. They probably would rob innocent people too, but in this case this guy wasn't really that hard.

It was during the US Open Tennis championships which

took place in Queens near Shea Stadium and this event would draw tourists from all over the country and world into NYC that would attend. It was a high profile event for the city and one that is protected in the concept of the city being a safe place to visit.

One family from the Midwest was in town for this event, it was two middle aged parents and their early 20s son Brian. They happened to be changing trains near the club Roseland on this fateful evening when they ran into this group and Darkstar pulled out a knife on them demanding their money. Now it is unclear how much Bobbie was actually involved in the incident or at all, sometimes it does happen that someone you are with just does something you completely did not expect. But either way he definitely had no part in what happens next.

Bobbie was by all accounts a really nice kid according to those that knew him at Bayside High School. My brother knew him well also, he worked at Sizzler with him.

Darkstar demands these people's money and their son Brian defends them stepping in front of his parents. A scuffle ensues and Darkstar stabs this kid in the chest killing him and they all run upstairs into the club for some reason. I'm sure no one there thought the kid Brian got badly hurt, and maybe they were high or drunk, but they go into the club.

Brian dies from the injuries and the police find this group upstairs in the club and arrest them.

This event was high profile so the city wants to make an

example of anyone that Darkstar knew in the group that night, regardless of whether or not they actually played any part in the robbery. It's a law called "Acting in concert" which would come up many times in my life. It means the person in the group that did nothing, or the least would receive the same most serious charge as the person that did the worst. In this case felony murder during a robbery. Of a tourist no less. This group was fucked.

Bobbie DeKamp was sentenced along with Darkstar to life in prison and wound up doing almost 30 years before finally being released not long ago. He had no part in the robbery or murder but got "Caught up" with the wrong crowd and situation and that moment defined his entire life.

As a father this type of thing terrifies me, I can't stress to my son enough to never be around any behavior that he thinks could even have the slight bit of inappropriateness or illegality, even in a wild guess of what could come. I hate to instill this kind of worry in him, but I have been caught up and know many that have been caught up and it ruined so many lives.

If you take anything away from this this book let it be this –

Don't get caught up.

Chapter 17

FUCKING QUEENS!

We started going to clubs in the 80's when I was 16 years old, right around 1987 and that in itself was an insane thought. The club seen in NYC in the 1980s into the early 1990s was probably the most lawless uninhibited explicit scene in the history of nightclubs and for under-age kids to be a part of the scene it blows my mind still today. They did not card for age, drugs were literally free for kids that didn't mind hanging out with slightly older men and women, sure you could ward off their sexual advances, but you had better keep your wits about you. Many a kid woke up in a situation where they had done things or weren't exactly sure what they had done, and with whom.

Crazy thought, right? But it was life, there are writers now, famous writers that "Turned tricks" too for money and drugs back then, but those are not my stories to tell. Many of the things I witnessed but did not explicitly participate in are not my stories to tell. My purpose in life and in this book is certainly not to expose a hidden part of someone else's life, that is between them and their own motivations.

Some big name graffiti writers were rats too, informants, and no I'm not talking about the ones that are called rats all over the place on social media, I'm talking about some heroes, people that used to rat and inform to the vandal squad in exchange for a pass to hit their local yards without risk. Again, not my stories to tell, the streets talked, always back then and it was known by those that were there who was doing what. Many people live with this information without sharing it, and maybe it wasn't even as big of a deal back then, it was survival mode for many in their own neighborhoods, maybe the temptation was too great, or maybe they were just jealous rats, I don't know or care anymore.

And the funny thing about cops, or maybe it was not so funny, if you told a cop something in confidence about someone back then, they couldn't wait to tell that person or others what you told them, that's just the way they were, out to turn the streets against themselves.

But I digress, as usual, now let's get back into the Dome AKA The Saint on 2nd Ave near St. Marks, c1987, not sure how we got in then, somebody knew somebody and we walked right in. It was on the cusp of closing for good in the next 6 months or so, hearing the stories of the place now it's pretty crazy, Keith Haring was there that night, others too I'm sure.

This was not the first time I had crossed paths with Keith, the most notable time was about 2 years earlier coming home late one night from Bronx Science with my brother.

It was winter 1985 and we were at Bronx Science a little late doing something after school, by the time we left it was almost 7pm and by the time we got to Times Square to change trains it was probably about 8pm or so. At the time, and still somewhat today, there were many foot tunnels connecting different parts of Times Square, many that were long and quiet after rush hour dies down and we were in one such connecting tunnel when we saw Keith up ahead doing one of his chalk drawings on the black backdrop where an ad once was. We immediately knew who it was and from about 40 meters away we yelled "Hey Freeze!" and made the police car chirping sounds which echoed loudly in the tunnel catching Keith by complete surprise. He immediately jumped up and started walking very briskly away from us, when we got to where he was we saw his unfinished drawing and tried to call out to him but he disappeared into the station.

Back in the Dome that night two years later, New Order "True Faith" was climbing the charts, shit was hot, I went with two rich 16 year old girls, both shall remain nameless, one from Riverdale and one from Parkslope Brooklyn, both went to top high schools, like myself.

We were discussing the meaning of life and future goals and the one from Riverdale could not get her mind around the fact that I had no plans and was making no early college selections, I couldn't see past 30 years old as my future, I didn't think or care if I lived past that. I cared about graffiti, music, robbing paint and just living my life in this crazy city in the moment.

We walked into the actual Dome part of the club on the top floor, which thinking back now was bright white across the top and "True Faith" was indeed playing at that exact moment. I had swallowed an unknown pill about 30 minutes earlier, it was all a dream, it was a movie looking back and that song will forever bring me right back to the walkthrough of that room with those two girls.

The rest of the night is so fuzzy unfortunately any attempt to describe the actual events would be purely fiction, on account of the unknown pill that I swallowed that a guy I knew there handed me when we walked in. But still that night resonates with me until this day as a moment of complete freedom and no fear of consequences or plans for the future.

In some ways that is the first part of us to die, the part that can actually just live in the moment easily forgetting about the horrors of the night before and not even thinking about the consequences of the future. Those years are short lived, we get maybe two of them as sentient beings on the cusp of adulthood and even those two years are peppered with moments of regret and planning for future life. Years where we are developed enough intellectually to really formulate an opinion and hypothesis about life without really fretting about what we NEED to do about what they want us to do.

Other times around then I'd meet up with some city friends at a bodega or some sort of late night open store in the Village. Sometimes it was at Grays Papaya, sometimes I'd go with Chino or by myself or with Tame my friend from my neighborhood and bombing partner.

There was a crew of kids that hung out there, Kings Team, or KT they were known as, writers there would include Braer, Cocer, Tampa, Saes, Veefer, Image and others. We would hang there and then roll out to mischief and clubs and stuff like that. Back then there wasn't always an agenda sometimes we would just walk the streets of Manhattan all night taking tags with cans or markers, or sometimes just being stupid.

There were a lot of street kids and writers I would link up with over the years and some were more solid kids and friends than others, some were more out for self and would only be around you if they wanted something or thought they could get over with you or on you in some way. But these kids were solid. Sometimes I would bring the Triple Fat Goose jackets down there and sell them, I sold them to a lot of writers, some famous ones, but here's the thing, not everyone was a man (or kid) of his word. Sometimes kids would take a jacket, tell me they'd pay me the $100 next time they saw me but never would, that was just part of the game. I racked so many of them it wasn't like I was going to enforce it or get someone to try to collect on that debt, it just wasn't worth the effort for something I could rack more of later.

Cocer once asked me for a jacket and I brought it there and he said he'd pay me next time. Sure enough the next week when I met up with them there he was not only wearing the jacket but the first thing he did was hand me a crisp $100 bill, a man of his word. And these were the types of dudes you knew you could count on.

Another time myself, Chino, Cocer, Braer and I think Veefer and a few others were in the club "the World" on Houston Street (Pronounced HOWston) on a Friday night. It was packed, crazy door scene but obv these kids had connections and we were let in. Full of bridge and tunnel partiers mostly in their 20's and 30's with a decent amount of Wall Street peppered in. We were getting fucked up, drinking and other stuff that you can imagine was taking place at popular New York City clubs in the 1980s. But we weren't the only ones, much, if not all of the older crowd was also blasted out of their minds and this one guy dragging a completely wasted girl across the dancefloor dropped his wallet right in the middle of the dance floor, right in front of us, and it was FAT. We all looked at it for a minute and then each other, before one of us (This is the part where some details aren't mine to tell) grabbed the wallet and ran off the dance floor with the rest of us running behind him. Many kids I met in the 1980s would have never let that wallet surface again in front of us, never mind split it equally between the 5 of us, but this guy did, he opened the wallet and there were stacks of hundreds inside he pulled them out, counted us each out $200 which was about an even split and chucked the wallet back onto the floor.

Now, of course, the right thing to do would've been to grab the drunk bastard and give him HIS money back, but you know what? We were all hustling trying to make it in this big city, this guy was rich and making money in our city, so by our sense of street logic we were entitled to his money. And honestly, when you are 17 years old and someone hands you $200 in cash in a club you didn't really get into the ethics of it, you just celebrated.

By the late 1980s and early 1990s Club USA, Tunnel, and Limelight became the hottest of the mega clubs. Enormous main rooms with several, sometimes hidden, sub-rooms with varying styles of music and vibes. As an example, around 1989 an artist Kenny Scharf created the "Kenny Scharf" room at the Tunnel which was a room with pink furry walls and furry furniture and when you were high AF being in one of these rooms was a trip.

Door scenes have been around since the 1970s. The hottest clubs had a velvet rope out front holding back a crowd that wanted to get in and the most obnoxious host/door person standing on the other side of it. They were sometimes in drag, sometimes in suit or just plain clothes and always either with a clipboard or with an assistant holding a clipboard. This clipboard was "The list" as it was referred to and dozens of desperate party seekers would be standing there screaming "Im on the list" and being ignored for the most part by the obnoxious doorperson. If you had to identify yourself as being on the list there was already a good likelihood you weren't getting in. Unless someone really special actually put you on there.

As clubs would wane in popularity and the next club became hot, the old club would then broaden its entry requirements and more people would gain access.

But the easiest way to get into Redzone, Club USA, Limelight, The Tunnel and more was to be popular with the club scene and actually know "Kenny" or whatever other person was the door person, and the more alternative and off beat your look was the more you belonged, pink hair, facial piercings, mohawks, weird fur jackets, all things that we commonly wore.

We eventually looked like, "freaks "as my dad would call us before finally pulling me aside one day when I came home after three days and throwing me against the wall exclaiming "Do you like girls or guys?!" I shrugged him off of me and kept walking right out the door, teenage angst at its finest.

At Limelight we were regulars by the early 1990s, Tunnel too, I had pink hair, Duel had green, or vice versa on any given night. We used to go in there, a building that actually was a beautiful Gothic church, and enter the main room to a flash of strobing lights and bass thumping club music that varied over the years from techno to house to whatever. Usually by the time we even got inside we were a mess of substances and if you were truly cool, the guy at the door handed you "Drink tickets" which meant you could get free drinks as a 17, 18, 19 year old kid. We would immediately get the drinks, all at once and get wasted, then smoke so much weed in one of the back rooms we would become one with the vibrating packed crowd of bodies pressed up against ours moving in unison to a deep bass with no other sounds even audible at this point.

Many nights someone did offer the random pill here too, and by then I often did not question it, it was ecstasy, or a quaalude, or a ruphenol, who remembers anymore? Who remembered then? That was the idea. It was hot and humid, shirts came off, the drugs elevated our temperatures and the overcrowding of the space way beyond the fire code elevated the temperature as well. Table service was not popular at this time, that is not why we were there, people went to clubs then to feel people and be touched and be a part of a moving mass of humanity and sexuality completely free of inhibition. You stood on packed dance floors, sometimes with your shirt off, most of the times sweating like a beast in a room that reeked of smoke, body odor, sweat and candy all while completely surrendering yourself to the driving bass that overtook your soul if you let it.

There was a mostly naked guy that used to run around in limelight on a walkway above the main room with a saddle on his back. Did I ever wind up on the saddle galloping around the club at 3 am, 18 years old without a clue or inhibition left? Sure, probably, at least I think I did, but what was reality back then vs what is reality now looking back is difficult to discern.

Duel used to try to look out for me too, he knew I had a childhood condition that made me susceptible to ODing on drugs, one time he saw a guy we knew trying to hand me a pill in the middle of the Limelight main dancefloor, he ran over and slapped it up in the air. I remember Duel yelling at the guy repeatedly over the loud music - "He's got a condition! Don't be giving him nothing!" And I'll never forget he did that for me, that's not to say many times when he didn't see, I did take that fucking pill.

Because my judgement was already shot on account of the alcohol, immaturity, desire, and whatever else was shoveled into our brains that particular day in terms of fights, stress, hate, etc., all things we were going to escape from no matter what.

Suddenly one night I was looking down at myself and Duel walking from up in the sky, I was out of my body, and when I looked at my heart I could see it beating about 10" outside of my chest, thumping harder and harder and things started to go silent. We were in our neighborhood, just randomly smoking a ton of marijuana at like 1am in a park, but I was on a medication at this time and my body still polluted on substances from the club night before. My ears rang and then ...silence ...

When it went silent I got scared, I also couldn't breathe, I yelled down to Duel from my perch on top of a street-light, he was so tiny from where I was although I was in actuality standing right next to him. I screamed at the top of my lungs so he could hear me "I need help I'm going to die" and started crying. I think I dropped to my knees on the floor; I can't remember what came next.

I woke up in the back of his car, he dragged me into an emergency room, leaving me in front of the staff, he turned to leave and they screamed at him "What happened?!"

Duel screamed back -

"I don't fucking know, HE SMOKED SOMETHING!"

Then ran out the door. And that is what you did, you weren't going to stick around for the police, what else could you do at this point? I once went to an emergency room with a broken arm and the police wanted to investigate my family for domestic violence.

But on this night my heart was beating more than 200 times per minute by now as I was fading to black. I thought I was having a heart attack.

I woke up hours later in a hospital room hooked up to IVs and monitors, my medical records today still mention that night, it simply reads "Unknown Narcotics incident and possible overdose." I was 20 years old, and they did not inform my parents or anyone else.

Two days later we went to the Tunnel and got fucked up,

you know that thing when you were a kid, or sort of a kid? You would say to your friends "Let's go out and get fucked up tonight!" and they would say "Fuck yeah" and it didn't matter? Gosh I miss that; I mean yeah it was not ideal what we were doing but it felt so good to just not worry about consequences which at some point is what life is all about.

Perhaps even crazier is that by the late 1980s we had driver's licenses and cars, and we used to drive sometimes to clubs and drive in states of mind that today would be ghastly, opening car doors at red lights to throw up from the driver's seat, closing the door and keep on driving. But here's the thing, Drunk Driving was barely a crime in the 1980s, I guess with the two thousand murders per year and all of the other quality of life problems the city had, drunk driving just wasn't on their radar. Sure it was technically illegal but I don't know a single person ever arrested for it until the mid 1990s. It would be very common to get pulled over by the police back then and have them pour out alcohol onto the floor if you were actually drinking while driving and then let you leave, or if you were too drunk to drive they would make someone else drive or take your keys and throw them on a nearby roof, stranding you and your vehicle in the middle of the street.

Sometimes they would rough you up, but inevitably it always ended with the cops leaving and you not being arrested. I got the sense it was not paperwork they wanted to do. Crazy right? It would be that way in parts of Europe for many years later, but that's another story altogether.

St. Marks was like a bizarre bazaar in the 1980's right near where it crossed second avenue. All of the city's junkies, homeless and thieves would set up blankets selling anything and everything they could get their hands on, purses, wallets, electronics, car radios, jewelry, drugs, you name it. The street was lined with vendors usually laid out on the floor on blankets with merchandise sprawled out. People were bartering for all kinds of shit, and late at night there were almost no regular citizens in sight, it was all of the dregs and the street kids that ran the city. I mean this was literally something out of a Blade Runner type dystopian future sci-fi story.

There was a taco stand on 2nd Ave just below St. Marks, on the same block called San Loco and until this day (It is still around someplace downtown I believe but not the same location) is the best tacos and burritos I have ever had, and I live in Los Angeles, still the best.

It was open 19 hours per day from like 10am until 5 am and needless to say all of the shit on the street spilled inside and there was always some violent drama going on. The guy that worked behind the counter had a baseball bat and often he would leap over the counter and show someone a whack or two as he kicked them out the door, fights often spilled out onto the street or from the street inside, and there was always some homeless junkie begging or crying for something in there.

But this was our city and we loved it, we just sat there and ate and watched the drama unfold. We used to call it "Late night dramatics" and almost every night out ended with us eating there at 4am, and we simply ask "Late night dramatics?" and everyone we were with knew that meant lets go get tacos.

As I mentioned, I had pink hair, or blue and Duel had green hair, both in fur coats and weird worker clothing that was popular with club kids at the time, we just ate and were standing on 2nd Ave at the light about to cross St. Mark's when a police cruiser was slowly rolling by with the windows down. This was the time when all New York City cops had black hair and black mustaches, and most were violent and angry and took the laws only as suggestions.

This cop is moving like one mile per hours as he drives six inches from me and Duel, the cop in the passenger seat looks right at us and says "Fucking Queens!"

Duel turns to me and says, "How does he know we are from Queens?"

"He doesn't know" I said, "He is calling us fucking queens."

Chapter 18

Redemption?

In 2007 I wrote two novels; one was loosely based on a true story when my brother and I were about twelve years old and coding and running services on what would eventually become the internet.

My brother was a known hacker at eleven years old and appeared on the television news, typing code in a story about kids and computers. There is a significant amount of overlap in that story with Gibson and Jimmy, the minibike, Fort Totten, and more with this book.

While I was editing that novel, I adapted it into a screenplay and it was optioned by several major Hollywood players just when the financial collapse of 2008 occurred.

The movie wound up not being made. But the "Notes" I received back from different producers and WGA writers always had one thing in common, there was a lack of accountability and growth that made the characters of the story not "Redeemable". Issues we wound up working out in rewrites and needed some fiction to accomplish.

This book is no different, reading through this anthology of short stories I realize that we are not redeemable characters as depicted in this book. That is just the nature of this kind of book, being short stories of a lifestyle and events that took place without a broader connection to us as people and what we became.

And that does trouble me a bit, knowing my own life, we did go on to accomplish some things, and be fulfilled and live a life that would be deemed a success by almost any metric, but as people, were we redeemable characters in this insane life we led growing up?

Were we products of our environment, innocent victims that survived the only way we knew how and had fun along the way? Or did we contribute to that environment helping to create and perpetuate a self-fulfilling prophecy and creating other, younger than us, products of this same environment?

And in a broader sense, I know we are redeemable, we never did anything to anyone that wasn't actively participating in our world, there were no true victims of any of our violence and anger, in fact we never perpetrated any violence or anger on anyone that wasn't already attempting violence on us.

But even being redeemable from the outside looking in, were we ever really redeemed on the inside in our own minds and hearts? Was there true redemption for any of us that participated in this life of old New York City, graffiti, clubs, etc.?

I don't think so.

It seems the vast majority of us exist now on Instagram, posting pictures and tales of the past or trying to continue to live a similar lifestyle and posting our every move for the world in the hope that it will know we still exist.

We long for the days we know are never coming back,

not out of nostalgia but out of a true discontentment
with the world we currently live in.

That may be more of a fault of the current world but
at the end of the day I don't feel redeemed or feel like
I have achieved true redemption. I pine for things and
lifestyles I no longer have and can never get back. I love
my life now but still define myself by the life I lived as a
child and teen.

There is no material success that can quench that thirst
for many of us.

Is that redemption?

I don't know.

FINAL THOUGHTS

Our New York City was a very raw tough place to live and come of age. Even today, living in New York City takes a toughness not required to grow up in other cities like Los Angeles where I now live and raise my own son.

There is a degree of vulnerability that comes with commuting by train, bus and foot vs. being locked in the safety and mobility of your own car and being able to get away from crowds at the end of your day. When I first moved to L.A. with my friend MB he remarked how little dedication it took for people to stand outside clubs here to get in during the winter.

And Old New York, "Our New York", was especially tough, because in addition to what I just mentioned, it was relatively lawless, you were on your own, there were almost 2000 murders per year at that time, in many instances no one was coming to save you. But there is one thing that disturbs me about the comparisons of life then vs life now, especially when it comes to the idea that we are safer now, that all of this technology and these laws have made us safer.

Sure, some of our innocence never really existed in Our New York, we saw and found out the most horrible and wonderful parts of life on our own. I myself, was the victim of attacks by pedophiles as a child and teen and learned to deal with and protect myself on my own, things that still stay in my mind almost every day of my life until today, things that very few know about.

But largely, all of the dangers I survived and was exposed to growing up in Old New York, were of my own doing, I put myself in many of those situations by living the life we led, it was our thing so to speak. And of the 2000 or so murders every year in NYC at that time, many of the victims fell into some part of that as well, they put themselves in a lifestyle that exposed themselves to danger.

And we survived or didn't, and it is always tragic when a human life is lost and never right to blame the victim of anything that happens to us. But like with Mob Violence in La Costra Nostra, it was their thing, they knew the risks when they chose that life. There were no true victims in the Mafia. And not a ton of true victims in our Old New York.

But to my hardest recollection, there were no groups of children slaughtered at school by the dozen. Murdered at school where they are supposed to be safe and learn about how to become productive members of their world, full of excitement and joy.

I may have lost my innocence as a child when I was exposed to disgusting sexual bullshit, or attacked on the subway when I was ditching school, but I never had to think about being slaughtered like fucking cattle at school. My son now does active shooter drills in his school.

And that affects his ability to go on and have HIS THING the way we had OUR THING. He has a sense of fear of the world and reality at 9 years old that we never did. He knows there is true evil out there, did we?

I can't remember thinking I knew what evil was at that age, else would I have been brave enough to take the train into the worst parts of the city at 3am by myself at 15 years old? I did what I had to do to survive but how could a child survive a school shooting? What could a child do to prepare to defend himself against a school shooter the way I did against a weirdo or rival graffiti writer? Can he carry mace and a bat? It's just not that simple now.

I didn't plan on putting anything like this in the book, but as I was editing it this horrible tragedy happened when a piece of garbage killed 19 young souls and 2 adults at school in Texas. How could I call myself a human being and be finishing a book and not mention this? Part of my motivation for writing the books I am writing is immortality, to have something exist long after I am gone -

Alexandria Aniyah Rubio, 10, Alithia Ramirez, 10, Amerie Jo Garza, 10, Annabell Guadalupe Rodriguez, 10, Eliahana Cruz Torres, 10, Eliana "Ellie" Garcia, 9, Eva Mireles, 44, Irma Garcia, Jackie Cazares, 10, Jailah, Nicole Silguero, 10, Jayce Luevanos, 10, Jose Flores, 10, Layla Salazar, 10, Makenna Lee Elrod, 10, Maite Rodriguez, Miranda Mathis, 11, Nevaeh Bravo, Rojelio Torres, 10, Tess Marie Mata, Uziyah Garcia, 10, Xavier Lopez, 10

That's them, the victims of unfathomable evil in the form of another human being. Their names should exist as often as possible, their lives were cut short, they never got to have their thing the way we had ours.

I have not prayed to a god since the 4th grade, I am not religious, but there must be a god because how else can we make sense of fucking life? Why is there evil? How could there be directly polarized good vs. evil if not created as such? I am praying now that there is a god, because politicians, Twitter, and all of the other bullshit in this world will never make sense of any of it.

I pray that these children and other true victims in this world find peace in another life.

I pray for everyone, all of you, and myself, let's all just do the best we can to make the world the best place we can and be kind and helpful to one another.

Thank you for reading this part of my journey, hope you liked it or were inspired by it. Document your own journey, we each only get one and before you know it you will have reached your destination.

And if you didn't like it, well that's just too damn bad, you'll get over it.

One love!

GLOSSARY

Bombing - The act of doing graffiti, usually in bulk

Buffed - Cleaned graffiti that usually leaves smudges and stains

Ding Dong - A type of train that makes a ding dong sound when the doors close

Caught Up - Get arrested and charged for a crime you might not have commited but you were there with someone that commited a crime

Esplanade - A well known place they parked trains near Morris Park in the Bronx

Flats - Trains with flat sides

Grabbed - Apprehended, usually by the cops

Gold Fronts - Gold Teeth worn in a mouthpiece over existing teeth

Hard Rock - a street tough guy that is fearless and will never back down

Halvsies - Left over paint that had about half left

Hatch - A yellow emergency exit trap door in the side-walk throughout the transit system. They were meant to evactuate trains but writers used these to access tunnels.

Krylon - A brand of paint

Lay-up - Parked trains in between stations when not in use, above ground or in a tunnel.

On the block - Where you hang out with your friends as informally as you want, on the block near where you lived

Piece - A more artistic piece of graffiti

Ridgie - Trains with ridges on the sides

RR (CC and others) - Express trains were sometimes designated by doubling the line name in the 1980s and previous. For example the R trains was known as the RR and so on, the MTA would put this double letter on the train marker

Rusto - A Brand of paint

Shaved Part - A barber would shave a hair part into a person's head

Throw-up - A bubble letter meant to quickly write a graffiti name en masse

Throw down - Fight an enemy

Toy - A graffiti writer that is not good or respected

CHRIS "STANE" ANTHONY is a writer, artist and father currently living in Los Angeles. He has had several screenplays optioned and is in the process of completing two novels. He has been keeping journals and writing prose since college and has many volumes of stories to share.